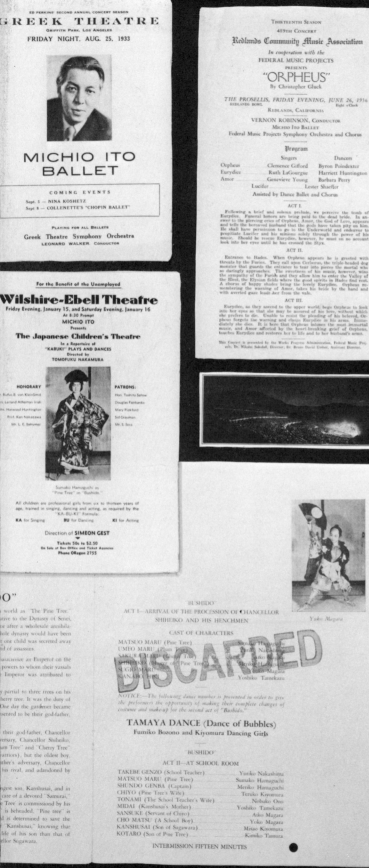

GREEK THEATRE

ED PERKINS' SECOND ANNUAL CONCERT SEASON

GRIFFITH PARK, LOS ANGELES

FRIDAY NIGHT, AUG. 25, 1933

MICHIO ITO
BALLET

COMING EVENTS

Sept. 5 — NINA KOSHETZ

Sept 8 — COLLENETTE'S "CHOPIN BALLET"

PLAYING FOR ALL BALLETS

Greek Theatre Symphony Orchestra

LEONARD WALKER, CONDUCTOR

For the Benefit of the Unemployed

Wilshire-Ebell Theatre

Friday Evening, January 15, and Saturday Evening, January 16

At 8:30 Prompt

MICHIO ITO

Presents

The Japanese Children's Theatre

In a Repertoire of

"KABUKI" PLAYS AND DANCES

Directed by

TOMOFUKU NAKAMURA

HONORARY:	PATRONS:
Mr. Rufus B. von Kleinsmid	Hon. Toshito Satow
Mrs. Leland Atherton Irish	Douglas Fairbanks
Prof. Harwood Huntington	Mary Pickford
Prof. Ken Nakazawa	Sid Grauman
Mr. L. E. Behymer	Mr. S. Sera

Sumako Hamaguchi as
"Pine Tree" in "Bushido."

All children are professional girls from six to thirteen years of age, trained in singing, dancing and acting, as required by the "KA-BU-KI" Formula.

KA for Singing   BU for Dancing   KI for Acting

Direction of SIMEON GEST

Tickets 50c to $2.50

On Sale at Box Office and Ticket Agencies

Phone ORegon 2755

"...O"

...world as "The Pine Tree."

...tive to the Dynasty of Senei,

...e after a wholesale annihila-

...hole dynasty would have been

...one child was secreted away

...d of assassins.

...characterize an Emperor on the

...powers to whom their vassals

...Emperor was attributed to

...y partial to three trees on his

...cherry tree. It was the duty of

...One day the gardener became

...sented to her god-father.

...their god-father, Chancellor

...versary, Chancellor Shiheiko,

...um Tree" and "Cherry Tree"

...arriors), but the oldest boy,

...ather's adversary, Chancellor

...his rival, and abandoned by

...gest son, Kanshusai, and in

...care of a devoted "Samurai,"

...e Tree is commissioned by his

...is beheaded. "Pine tree" is

...s determined to save the

..."Kanshusai," knowing that

...life of his son than that of

...ellor Sugawara.

THIRTEENTH SEASON

459TH CONCERT

Redlands Community Music Association

In cooperation with the

FEDERAL MUSIC PROJECTS

PRESENTS

"ORPHEUS"

By Christopher Gluck

THE PROSELLIS, FRIDAY EVENING, JUNE 26, 1936

REDLANDS BOWL   Eight o'Clock

REDLANDS, CALIFORNIA

VERNON ROBINSON, CONDUCTOR

MICHIO ITO BALLET

Federal Music Projects Symphony Orchestra and Chorus

Program

	Singers	Dancers
Orpheus	Clemence Gifford	Byron Poindexter
Eurydice	Ruth LaGourgue	Harriett Huntington
Amor	Genevieve Young	Barbara Perry
Lucifer		Lester Shaefier

Assisted by Dance Ballet and Chorus

ACT I.

Following a brief and solemn prelude, we perceive the tomb of Eurydice. Funeral honors are being paid to the dead bride. In answer to the piercing cries of Orpheus, Amor, the God of Love, appears and tells the bereaved husband that the gods have taken pity on him. He shall have permission to go to the Underworld and endeavor to propitiate Lucifer and his minions solely through the power of his music. Should he rescue Eurydice, however, he must on no account look into her eyes until he has crossed the Styx.

ACT II.

Entrance to Hades. When Orpheus appears he is greeted with threats by the Furies. They call upon Cerberus, the triple-headed dog monster that guards the entrance to tear into pieces the mortal who so daringly approaches. The sweetness of his music, however, wins the sympathy of the Furies and they allow him to enter the Valley of the Blest, the Elysian fields where the good spirits in Hades find rest. A chorus of happy shades bring the lovely Eurydice. Orpheus remembering the warning of Amor, takes his bride by the hand and with averted gaze leads her from the vale.

ACT III.

Eurydice, as they ascend to the upper world, begs Orpheus to look into her eyes so that she may be assured of his love, without which she prefers to die. Unable to resist the pleading of his beloved, Orpheus forgets the warning and clasps Eurydice in his arms. Immediately she dies. It is here that Orpheus intones the most immortal music, and Amor affected by the heart-breaking grief of Orpheus, touches Eurydice and restores her to life and to her husband's arms.

This Concert is presented by the Works Progress Administration, Federal Music Projects, Dr. Nikolai Sokoloff, Director; Dr. Bruno David Ussher, Assistant Director.

BUSHIDO

ACT I—ARRIVAL OF THE PROCESSION OF CHANCELLOR

SHIHEIKO AND HIS HENCHMEN

CAST OF CHARACTERS

MATSUO MARU (Pine Tree)	Sumako Hamaguchi
UMEO MARU (Plum Tree)	Meriko Nakashima
SAKURA MARU (Cherry Tree)	Yukiko Miya
SHIHEIKO (Enemy of Pine Tree)	Meriko Hayakawa
SUGO MARU	Yoko Magara
SANABO CHO	Yoshiko Tamekazu

NOTICE:—The following dance number is presented in order to give the performers the opportunity of making their complete changes of costume and make-up for the second act of "Bushido."

TAMAYA DANCE (Dance of Bubbles)

Fumiko Bozono and Kiyomura Dancing Girls

BUSHIDO

ACT II—AT SCHOOL ROOM

TAKEBE GENZO (School Teacher)	Yuriko Nakashima
MATSUO MARU (Pine Tree)	Sumako Hamaguchi
SHUNDO GENBA (Captain)	Meriko Hamaguchi
CHIYO (Pine Tree's Wife)	Teruko Kiyomura
TONAMI (The School Teacher's Wife)	Nobuko Ono
MIDAI (Kanshusai's Mother)	Yoshiko Tamekazu
SANSUKE (Servant of Chiyo)	Aiko Magara
CHO MATSU (A School Boy)	Yoko Magara
KANSHUSAI (Son of Sugawara)	Mitao Kiyomura
KOTARO (Son of Pine Tree)	Kimiko Tamura

INTERMISSION FIFTEEN MINUTES

Yuko Magara

The Japanese Theatre Association, Inc.

Presents

TOKUJIRO TSUTSUI

and his Company of Players from the ...... Theatre, Osaka

D0793686

....

...erican stage

Michio Ito

Settings by Ryu

All scenes take place during the Genroku Period, early eighteenth century

at the

Figueroa Playhouse

940 SOUTH FIGUEROA STREET

Los Angeles, California

ONE WEEK ONLY

beginning Monday evening, February 10, 1930

MICHIO ITO

presents

A Series of Dance Compositions

and

Plays for Dancers

at the

Argus Bowl

1805 Hill Drive   Eagle Rock

Maude Howard, Pianist

PROGRAM

For Monday Evening, September 2, 1929, at 9 o'Clock

1.	Andante Cantabile	BEATRIX BAIRD, DOLORES LOPEZ, DOROTHY WAGNER	Tschaikowsky
2.	Tango	MICHIO ITO	Albeniz
3.	El Gaucho	EDITH JANE, Choreography by EDITH JANE	Strickland
4.	Habanera	BEATRIX BAIRD	Sarasate
5.	Spanish Fan Dance	DOLORES LOPEZ	Sarasate
6.	Kyo No Shiki	HAZEL WRIGHT	Yamada
7.	Javanese Dance	XENIA ZARINA	Kelly
8.	Siva-Siva	LESTER HORTON, KATHERINE STUBERGH, Choreography by LESTER HORTON	Cohen
9.	Burmese Umbrella Dance	ANNE DOUGLAS, Choreography by ANNE DOUGLAS	Ketelby
10.	Burmese Temple Dance	MICHIO ITO, EDITH JANE, ARNOLD TAMON	(Burmese)

INTERMISSION (5 Minutes)

11.	Somebody-Nothing, a Kyogen or ancient Japanese farce		
	translated by	MICHIO ITO and LOUIS V. LEDOUX	
	Master	Ralph Matson	
	Tarakaja	Lester Horton	
	Girokaja	Thomas De Graffenried	

INTERMISSION (3 Minutes)

12.	Balloon Dance	LILLIAN POWELL, Choreography by LILLIAN POWELL	Zamecnik
13.	Tone Poems (Oto No Nagare) No. 1 and 2	MICHIO ITO	Yamada
	No. 3	DOROTHY WAGNER	
14.	Preludes Opus No. 11 No. 5	BEATRIX BAIRD	Scriabine
	No. 6	ARNOLD TAMON	
	No. 8	DOROTHY WAGNER	
	No. 9	EDITH JANE	
	No. 10	XENIA ZARINA	
15.	Caresse Dansee	DOROTHY WAGNER	Scriabine
16.	Little Shepherdess	HAZEL WRIGHT	Debussy
17.	Arabesque	ANNE DOUGLAS, MICHIO ITO, LILLIAN POWELL	Debussy

All choreography by MICHIO ITO with the exceptions noted

Company Manager	Paul Nidate
Stage Manager	Lewis Barrington
Assistants	Peggy Jones, Toyo Miyatake

Friday Evening, September 20th, at 7:30 o'Clock

in the Rose Bowl, Pasadena

A COMMUNITY DANCE FESTIVAL

with over 200 dancers

under the direction of

Michio Ito

MICHIO ITO

MICHIO ITO

The Dancer and His Dances

Helen Caldwell

UNIVERSITY OF CALIFORNIA PRESS • BERKELEY • LOS ANGELES • LONDON

FRONTISPIECE:

"He was able, as he rose from the floor, . . . or as he threw out an arm, to recede from us into some more powerful life." W. B. Yeats on Michio Ito

Permission to reproduce copyrighted material has been granted by: M. B. Yeats, Miss Anne Yeats, and The Macmillan Company of London & Basingstoke (for two lines from *The Collected Poems of W. B. Yeats,* copyright 1933); Macmillan Publishing Company, Inc. of New York (for two lines from "Upon a Dying Lady" by William Butler Yeats, copyright 1919 by Macmillan Publishing Co., renewed 1947 by Bertha Georgie Yeats); Faber and Faber Ltd and New Directions Publishing Corporation (for three lines from *The Cantos of Ezra Pound,* copyright 1948 by Ezra Pound); Manchester University Press, and Barnes and Noble (for illustrations in D. J. Gordon et al., *Yeats Images of a Poet,* copyright 1961); J. T. Caldwell (for all drawings, programs, posters, and photographs reproduced throughout this book and not attributed to other sources).

University of California Press
Berkeley and Los Angeles, California

University of California Press, Ltd.
London, England

ISBN: 0-520-03219-5
Library of Congress Catalog Card Number: 76-7756
Copyright © 1977 by The Regents of the University of California

Designed by Kadi Karist Tint

Printed in the United States of America

1 2 3 4 5 6 7 8 9 0

For Jonathan Trumbull Caldwell

Contents

Preface

The dancer Michio Ito, whose talents were admired by Debussy and Rodin in Paris, by Yeats and Shaw in England, and by thousands in the United States, was born in Tokyo on 13 April 1892(?). On 6 November 1961 he died in his native city, where he had resided since 1942.

Although Ito's paternal grandfather was a samurai who opposed the entrance of the West into Japan, his father, Tamekichi, was an architect of the new school and a friend of Frank Lloyd Wright. His mother, Kimiye Iijima, daughter of a well-known zoologist, was a woman with advanced ideas. Michio described his parents as "a kind of modern boy and girl," who generously helped their seven sons to careers, each of his own choosing. All seven entered artistic professions. Michio, the eldest, at age eighteen set forth from Tokyo to explore Europe's art. At twenty-two he became a professional dancer.

The present study is intended to describe his dances and shed light on the nature of his art. For this reason, mention of all things and persons unrelated to that art have been rigidly excluded. The reader will not find here the salacious anecdote and dreary curbstone Freud so popular in pseudo biographies of our time. This is an unpretentious study in aesthetics dedicated to a genius.

My credentials for this work are thirteen years of earnest study under Michio Ito, from 1929 through 1941—the time of his residence in Los Angeles—together with previous and later research centered on Greek tragedy and English drama.

x   *Michio Ito*   *1931*   *Photograph by Toyo Miyatake*

In the autumn of 1972 the motion-picture photographer Hal Mohr, and his wife Evelyn Venable, convinced me that I should allow him to film my performance of some of Ito's solo dances, if only for a record of the choreography. Twenty-seven dances were so recorded—in practice tunic, on black and white film, to music—and a more ambitious plan was conceived for these and other dances of Ito's composition to be filmed in color with proper costumes and under more favorable conditions. My book was begun as a script to accompany these films and will, I hope, ultimately serve that purpose.

An objection will perhaps be made that the book ends abruptly, with World War II. War is abrupt. Concentration camps are abrupt. As I state and firmly believe, Michio Ito's life as a great universal artist ended with Pearl Harbor. When I saw him in the nineteen-fifties, he would say nothing of the postwar Japanese theater in which he had been and was even then active. He was more interested in the little fact that I continued to practice, and meditate upon, his old dances. And I feel now that he then believed I would somehow preserve those dances as they should be preserved. He always had more confidence in my abilities than they warranted.

It is a pleasure to express my gratitude to our University Research Library for its excellent, ever-willing assistance; and my warm thanks to the staff at University of California Press at Los Angeles, who, as always, have put forth every effort to give this little book a fine dress.

A special note of appreciation goes to Michio Ito's friend, the re-nowned artist-photographer Toyo Miyatake, who generously contributed his beautiful pictures to enhance and illustrate the book's thought.

I wish to thank, also, others who have cheered me on in one way and another: Barbara Perry, Cecilia Nakamura, Roberta Nixon, Teizo Taya, Elena Beattie, T. Scott Miyakawa, and last but not least Ensho Ashikaga whose calligraphy adorns the title page.

H. C.

University of California
Los Angeles

MICHIO
ITO

I The Dance Poems of Michio Ito

Is dancing art? As long as it expresses an idea—yes. Nothing, however, is art without an idea behind it.

Those are the words of Michio Ito, master choreographer of our century. Although his great symphonic choreographies have for the most part, I fear, been lost, so too the dances composed for plays and operas, at least forty shorter compositions have been saved—all, with one exception, intended for solo performance.[1] Each of these compositions embodies a different idea, each is wrought about a single mood. Yet all are variations on the one dramatic theme of love in its struggle with an opposite: life with death, creation with destruction, harmony with war, good with evil, and so on.

Frequently, as in ancient Greek drama, it is individual man who finds himself in the presence of some universal force—outside or within him—sometimes contending against it, sometimes making peace with it, adoring it, or mingling his own spirit with it. The dance entitled *Ball*, for example, might seem a simple game in which the dancer rejoices in an instinctive joy of movement as he throws an imaginary ball to an invisible player (or players) and receives it in return, if it were not that we, as spectators, experience a feeling of exultation laced with a pleasurable sense of peril. And we suddenly recognize that this is no ordinary ball game, or even an impression of a ball game. Who or what is the invisible player? Fate? The "whips and scorns of time"? The ugly devils of everyday existence? Who is the visible player, so sure of his own grace and dexterity that he makes light of the game's hazards and finally relinquishes the ball in an almost nonchalant gesture of farewell? For what stakes is he playing?[2]

The initial conception for this dance came to Ito as he sat in the grandstand of a baseball park in New York City. It was a bright sunny day, he said, blue sky, crisp air, a slight breeze, and the players warming up below with rhythmic pitch and catch. As he sat watching the players and in happy anticipation of the game, the music of Chopin's Nocturne in F-sharp began to run through his head.* Out of the music's thought gradually (for Ito did not compose extempore) grew the visible patterned thought we call a dance. Although this dance evokes the sensuous pleasure of that moment at the ball park—sky, wind, the players' rhythms, the artist's emotion—it transcends that mood and, in harmony with Chopin's *idea*, lifts us into a higher realm, an elation of spirit where mind is also satisfied.

The subject matter or fable of Ito's dances is always brief, always simple, almost nothing as here—a ball thrown and caught, only that—but the mood, the idea, is grand. Laurence Binyon tells of a Japanese painter who "could give the effect of ten thousand miles of country on a fan."[3] Such miracles of evocation are also Ito's. *Ecclesiastique*, a dance lasting scarcely more than a minute and a half, an interpretation of a Schumann étude, has for its whole subject matter figures of a stained-glass window moving in the continuous formal gesture of one dancer, gesture perfectly controlled by the music. But what does the spectator see in his *mind's* eye? The whole story of the Fall: the angels in revolt around the throne of God, the serpent's guile, ministers of vengeance, the flight from the garden and its loss "till one greater Man restore us" with his love; or he may see whatever rises from his memory's depths to dress the stage with the age-old battle against evil that ends in good's triumph.

In Ito's dance poems (that is what he called them) music regulates and controls the movement. As Dalcroze stated, gesture in itself is nothing. Its whole value depends on the emotion, the idea, that inspires it.[4] A dance, then, in Ito's definition, is the music's idea rendered visible; and this

4   *Full titles of the music interpreted by these dances are given in Appendix 1.

visible form *is* the "poem," is the idea; and it is movement. The poets have long known of this truth, which Archibald MacLeish sums up as follows: "A poem is not the perfected expression of a predetermined thought but is itself the process of its thinking moving from perception to perception, sense to sense."[5] In the same way, Ito's dance poems are continuous movement, gesture moving inevitably into gesture, and a briefly held gesture within a dance serving only to punctuate the movement's meaning.

Nor does the movement, that is, the dance, end with the final gesture or pose at its conclusion. Ito's final gesture is never final; it merely enters the spectator's mind, where it beckons the imagination into the future. As the Chinese say of poetry, "The sound stops, the sense flows on."[6] This effect is perhaps most strongly felt in the interpretations of the Yamada tone poems and the Scriabin preludes, pieces in which the music itself seems to end with a questioning hint of something to come. *Tone Poem II,* for example, has as its idea the love-hate theme along with a fable of sin and revolt. A rebel who repents before a supreme magistrate cannot find the sheltering warmth of human companionship, or even forgiveness. On all sides he is pursued by men's vengeance and a god's indifference. He turns on his tormentors, then pleads but is repulsed. At last he rises against the harsh judgment; and the dance ends in a submission that turns out to be no submission at all but an imprecation upon society and its god—a gesture of hatred and defiance that grows more menacing in the darkness after the lights are extinguished. For the spirit of Prometheus is not dead, the spirit of Adam is not dead; that "ancient instinct of resistance to authority" resides in the depths of all our natures.[7]

The life of this dance's "final gesture" in our imaginations is eons longer than the dance itself, which in actual time lasts less than a minute and a half. All Ito's dance poems continue on in the infinite space of the human imagination. All are brief in themselves. *Tone Poem I* lasts scarcely more than a minute, but it too has an infinite life in the mind. Although it is a kind of companion piece to *Tone Poem II,* the mood is different. The fable is of an Eve, or a Miranda, in startled wonder before a "brave new world." Nature? Life? Love? Or are they the same? She flees from the strange phenomenon; attracted, she cautiously advances toward it; shrinks back; once more advances, this time resolutely, and with

Michio Ito in Yamada Tone Poem II   1926

6

dignity and joy herself offers to join the new element. Love has triumphed over fear; and the final gesture, if continued, would lift her into who knows what realms? *Tone Poem II* leaves the spectator with a feeling of admiration for human daring and an exultant sense of victory. With *Tone Poem I* there is an added surge of indescribable joy.

Faun (Tone Poem III), though light and humorous, also has an unfinished final gesture, but of a different sort. Here the idea is a silly vanity, a harmless self-love. Like the music, the dance pokes fun at the oversexed, bibulous half man, half beast, of ancient myth. There is no wildness in this faun, no sexuality, only the innocent vainglory of youth. Part fawn, he displays his beauty and accomplishments in an attempt to attract the attention of the Sun, who sits above in high indifference. The faun assumes attitudes, leaps with ridiculous grace, shoots an arrow into the Sun's countenance, another into the ground, washes his face with catlike elegance. The Sun sits on unseeing as before. The faun stretches in bored weariness, or pretended weariness, over the business. The last gesture: his head falls on his hand in sleep, or is he only pretending sleep? If one touched his eyelid, would he bound again into the endless round of his vain repertory?

In the telling, this dance may give the impression of a pantomime, but it is not. The straight lines of the floor pattern and of the unbroken movement change any suggestion of realism into a metaphor of the idea—human folly—at which the spectator laughs with the special inner satisfaction that comes only when we laugh at ourselves.

Scriabin's pull on our imagination is just as strong as Yamada's but it is more subtle, as a lyric poem can be more subtle and penetrate our spirit more deeply than a drama. In the dance poems to Scriabin's preludes, as in the music, we find predominant the artist's eternal desire to create order out of the chaos of nature.[8] Alfred Swan has written about the "marvelous structural symmetry" of these preludes.[9] The formal beauty of the dances conforms to that of the music. Their idea, in one form or another, reflects Hindu thought, although this is not necessarily true of the particular fable. For example, Ito liked to clothe *Prelude V* in the costume of a medieval page who goes to church to worship his patron saint. There he finds many holy images, each more holy than the one before. He does reverence to them all in turn; meanwhile with rising exaltation he gradually makes his way to his own saint's shrine, where he opens its doors, pushes aside the inner curtain, and joins his divinity in a great culminating gesture of adoration. Any fable, however, would do. The idea goes far beyond time and place, the idea that love increases with loving and the attendant joy grows in like proportion, with perhaps the added Vedic thought that man may achieve knowledge through devotion to a supreme being or ideal.

This and a related thought permeate *Prelude X*, whose idea contains evil also. The finite and the infinite are locked in their eternal strife, with the finite aspiring through force to be infinite. But, with its last gesture of soaring ecstatic love, this dance too looks toward the promised union with the infinite.

Prelude VI's idea is a fierce, joyous kind of love full of daring and devotion: the love of a warrior in a mysterious ceremonial battle for his lord, before whom he lays victorious spoils in a gesture of proud humility. It could be Arjuna of blameless life, the Persian Suhrab, a knight of the Crusades, or any hero fighting on behalf of a splendid cause.

Both fable and idea in *Prelude IX* are Siva, the dancing force that stirs the universe, god of love and hate, of creation and destruction, and of rebirth—the benevolent and sinister power of Nature. In symbolic gesture the fable runs: Siva sows men and all living things and infuses them with life's fire; but then he sows seeds of destruction and death, shoots arrows of plague, and with his might and fire brings low what men have built. Once more he sows the seeds of life in the four corners of the earth and adds thereto his fire signature, which can also mean life-giving warmth and the spirit of intelligence.

Like the other preludes, *Prelude VIII* has a strong flavor of divinity and formal ceremony. It is a kind of hymn to the sun, in which Dawn, or the goddess of dawn, pushes away the darkness to the left and to the right, that is, the past and the future, to disclose the bright sky of the present. She spreads abroad the dew and opens heaven's gates to the Sun's chariot, wakes the things of earth—breezes, butterflies,[10] men—and farewells the day with a gesture that has more of promise than farewell. For "dawn" is a radiant metaphor in any language, and this dance lightens the heart with man's most cherished emotion, hope, the only gift Pandora kept for us.

Ito's interpretation of Scriabin's *Caresse Dansée* is just that: love's caress in a highly stylized dance form. Technically, its floor pattern is confined and simple with the whole dance concentrated in symbolic movement of head, arms, and shoulders, gestures that thrust away the petty and personal to reveal a love that holds the universe within it. Scriabin wrote in his notebook: "I create the world by my caress."[11] This is the burden of Ito's dance poem, in which the small, gentle gesture of proffered love, the whispered confidence, the reticent greeting, raise the lover to their essence in the heaven of his spirit and become the Creator's all-embracing caress. Again, we see, it is the idea that is grand, although a fable of particular love evoke memories and allusions to recreate in us the idea's ecstasy.

Yeats wrote: "All the great masters have understood that there cannot be great art without the little limited life of the fable, which is always the better the simpler it is, and the rich, far-wandering, many-imaged life of the half-seen world beyond it."[12] In similar vein, Arthur Machen considered lyric poetry "the highest art because it is almost pure idea."[13] And Santayana explains this view with an analogy. We live, he says, in the fleeting moment, and to this fleeting moment "the poet is actually confined. [He] must enrich it with his endless vistas, vistas necessarily focused . . . in the eye of the observer here and now. . . . Is not the poetic quality of phrases and images due to their concentrating and liberating the confused promptings left in us by a long experience? When we feel the poetic thrill, is it not that we find sweep in the concise and depth in the clear, as we might find all the lights of the sea in the water of a jewel?"[14]

A fine illustration of such poetic power is found in Fernando Pessoa's verses about O Infante, the Portuguese Prince Henry whose fostering of navigational science gave birth to the great discoveries by Perestrelo, Vasco da Gama, Columbus, Magellan, and the rest:

Deus quere, o homem sonha, a obra nasce.
Deus quiz que a terra fosse toda uma,
Que o mar unisse, já não separasse,

which may be literally translated as

God wills, man dreams, the work is born.
God willed that the earth be one,
That the seas unite and no longer separate.

Compressed into those three lines are divine purpose, man's great works

Ito in Caresse
1926

and mind, and whole millennia of superstitious feeling that a god created the seas to separate the races of men, that it was a flying in the face of Providence to venture on the sea. In Pessoa's Portuguese we hear the persistent hissing of the sea, a thunderous beat of waves, and moaning wind; and our imagination soars above the discoverers' sails into the dark unknown, and beyond to new worlds. Through it all we feel Pessoa's idea: man's unity in God's loving plan.

In this poem, as in Ito's dances, fable and idea are inseparable elements of a continuous movement "from perception to perception, sense to sense," as MacLeish says; and the form so achieved *is* the poem, which brings the reader [spectator] into "a vision of reality that satisfies the whole being."[15] This "reality," whether of poem or dance, is universal, not particular like its fable. It is the artist's vision of reality but it is not a personal reality. Artistic dances, like great lyrics, are objective. Ito, for example, never "expressed himself" in his dances. Rather, they bring to life ideas and emotions common to all men, even though as perceived or felt by the artist. To quote Yeats again: "All that is personal soon rots; it must be packed in ice and salt," and, he added, "ancient salt [i.e., traditional form, traditional idea, traditional fable] is best."[16]

The salt and ice of the dances described above are ancient and traditional, but the tradition is not necessarily that of dance. In such compositions Ito seldom went to traditional dance for either idea or fable, or form: in the main, both the idea and its symbolic expression derive from other arts, as painting, sculpture, music, and above all from literature in its many genres, whether poetic, dramatic, philosophic, or mystical. For some dances, however, Ito did draw on traditional dances and used music inspired by such dances, for example, *Pavane, Minuet, Habanera,* and the like. Although the dances of this type breathe with the spirit of an age, they do not properly belong to fixed times or places. *Minuet* does not purport to be a real minuet, even though its subtle movement makes us feel minuet in our bones, all the minuets we have ever seen or heard or danced. Besides, it brings before us in a new visual form the metaphoric meaning of the word "minuet." We see in living movement the court of Louis XV as we know it from art and literature; but that is only the fable that goes hand in hand with the tight-laced idea, the idea of a lightly cynical formality repressing a loving nature, of elegant but calculated gesture symbolizing the cautious intrigue beneath a frivolous toilette of silks and silver lace.

Passepied also comes to us from the court of France but its fable is freer, more innocent, deriving as it does from Brittany's fisherfolk. A woman's buoyant love does show itself; the court is momentarily wished away and nature near. Although there is none of the robustness of the rude original, there is abandon; but it is the correct, self-conscious abandon of a Watteau shepherdess or a Fragonard.

Pavane is a noble's dance, one danced by ladies at the court of Henry VIII. As in *Passepied* and *Minuet,* there is in *Pavane* the same bending of emotions to fit stiff attitudes and cold ceremony; but here the pulse of life beneath the heavy silk is much stronger. The slow, steady throbbing of a human heart is suggested in the dancer's first gesture; and since the movement, as in all Ito's dances, is continuous, this heartbeat is felt throughout and continues in our ears after the vision has passed. Mean-

11

while, with the wide pattern of steps, grand gestures of arm and head, and slow ceremonial quality, our lady becomes larger than life: she is a goddess, a great goddess, and her dance, simple as it is, beats with the rhythm of the universe.

Spanish Fan is also danced with cold formality by a lady of high degree. Her steps, however, are more gentle than those of the older court dances described above; her dress, though opulent and grand in its proportions, is of soft lace, and a woman's gentleness does show through the subtle gesture of one brief phrase, later repeated. It is the ever-present fan that conveys the constriction and hard brilliance of court society, the fan with its incisive, at times almost menacing, suggestion of revolt beneath the monotonous pattern of a Spanish woman's life.

Javanese Dance partakes of traditional form and of court elegance, but, consonant with the lightness and frivolity of the music, this dance is scarcely serious. Like *Faun,* it is a show of innocent vanity and of charming flirtatiousness that blends with springtime blossoms; it is all outward grace, with only a hint of the inner beauty that selfless love bestows.

Although Ito went to traditional dance for the steps and gestures of *Habanera, Caucasian Dance,* and *Tango,* they are no more "authentic" or "ethnic" than the court dances. They derive from popular tradition and hence are closer to instinctive sex expression, but closer only by a shade and for a purpose. The first two, *Caucasion Dance* and *Habanera,* are borrowed from professional dances of the people—nautch and flamenco—dances that in their original form are lively, robust, and aggressive, displaying for money a frank, agile lubricity combined with the debased magic of ancient ceremony. Ito, in both dances, confined this flamboyance within the clear-cut movement of a formal design, at once making the dance a thing of irony and giving it allure and mystery. For he well knew that beauty, or even sexual attraction, is most potent when not completely revealed.

Tango is also an expression of earthy sex, but again with a difference; traditional gesture is again made to serve the idea. Ito once laughingly called his "a well-behaved tango," for its strength and beauty reside in its restraint. The sharp, formal floor pattern with its straight lines, the formal, tightly controlled gesture of the dancer, who appears ready to spring, ready to grasp, but does not, project us beyond the present moment into the shadowy landscape of the imagination, where, perhaps, the volcano will erupt in flaming lava.

Impression of a Chinese Actor was inspired not by traditional dance but by a related art form, the ancient Chinese theater: warriors both male and female, on horseback and afoot, lords and ladies making delicate love or chasing butterflies, coquettish ladies adept with sword or dagger to slit a bothersome lover's throat, prayer and temple bells, fantastic stage conventions, exploits and threatening stance as told in graceful gesture by a returning hero to his love—in a word, the flowery kingdom of our dreams caught in a decorative pattern that moves with the power of life.

Since Michio Ito was born in Japan and lived there to the age of eighteen, it might reasonably be supposed that the Japanese dances—*A Pair of Fans, Single Fan, Spring Rain,* and *Japanese Spring Dance*—derived from Japanese dance tradition. Actually they are no more exclusively Japanese than *Habanera* is flamenco. As in all Ito's compositions, it is the idea that dominates, that determines gesture, mood, and even fable. Of the four, *Spring Dance* is perhaps the most Japanese. Here we see conventional symbols of spring: breezes, budding trees, snow on sacred Fuji, processional, and other tokens of Japanese dance. It is a poem where nature and art meet in perfect geometric synthesis. Although we glimpse a beautiful old Japan, namely, the luxurious Genroku period, this dance is the most calm, the least emotional, of all Ito's works, finding its idea in a formal decorative design. It is the design itself that causes the spectator's feelings of pleasure and satisfaction, for here design and idea are synonymous: man moves harmoniously within the larger order of nature; this is the design; this is the idea. And it is the perfection of the design which animates a superficial, bygone day, raising it into the realm of universal idea.

In *Single Fan* both fable and idea are related to Japan's golden past, but the idea is directly expressed by the gestures themselves as well as by their overall pattern. The first two gestures (to a musical phrase of seven and a half measures) push aside the shadows of past and future to welcome into the present a figure out of time. With the initial gesture of the second phrase a samurai steps forth alive. With his fan, which is only incidentally a fan, he can suggest a sword, a shield, a mountain, a tree's foliage, a letter. He embodies not only the warlike exploits for his lord but also courtly pastimes of love and poetry and worship of nature's

13

OPPOSITE PAGE:
Ito in *Tango* costume
1926
INSERT:
Ito as Pierrot
LEFT:
Ito in *Tango* costume
Photograph by Toyo Miyatake   15

一千九百卅五年五月廿六日（日曜）午後八時半
ローズベルトハイスクール講堂に於て
（東第四街ごフィケット街）

南加日本語學園協會主催

ミチオ イトウ

舞踊の夕

ABOVE LEFT: Ito in Tango   1931   Photograph by Toyo Miyatake

ABOVE RIGHT: Ito in Tango   1935
Advertisement for program sponsored by the
Japanese School Association, Los Angeles

beauty in cherry blossom and fall leaf, and, above all, the samurai virtues of daring and devotion along with the wisdom and sweetness that come from self-conquest.[17] As the dance began with a dispelling of temporal mists, it ends with a double symbolic gesture that looks to past, present, and future, then to the future alone as the samurai resumes his place on time's frozen plain.

As fable, *Spring Rain* is a Japanese print come to life for a moment in new colors: a young man (or maiden) folding and opening his umbrella at the whim of the weather, displaying his many-colored finery to April's soft rain and sun. As idea, it is a brief thing of innocent vanity: youth's evanescent beauty ready to shield itself from life's showers with a huge, many-splendored paper umbrella.

Like the umbrella in *Spring Rain*, the two identical fans held in the hands of a single dancer play a certain role in *A Pair of Fans*. The fan is a Taoist symbol of flight toward the land of the immortals.[18] And we do find in this dance intimations of heavenly travel; but there are other elements present. The musical composition Ito interpreted was by his friend Kōsaku Yamada and supposedly based on an accompaniment to a fourteenth-century Noh dance entitled *Crane and Tortoise (Tsuru Kame)*.[19] The Japanese regard both crane and tortoise as symbols of a happy longevity. The crane is also a symbol of purity, in particular of fidelity, and a symbol of immortality. The idea of *A Pair of Fans* embraces all those ideals in the one ideal, conjugal love. As we of the West watch this dance, it may bring to mind Ovid's tale, "Philemon and Baucis."[20] We will see in its movement the loving old couple whose blameless life, mutual devotion, and piety saved them from the common fate of mankind, bestowing upon them a long life of happiness, followed by their wished for "death in the same hour," and a dual immortality, for they were changed into "two trees growing from a single trunk." Indeed, the dance's final gesture—the spread fans held aloft by the half-kneeling dancer—seems to represent the double foliage of that single tree. Another Noh play, *Takasago*,[21] appears to be more closely related to Ito's dance than *Crane and Tortoise* does. Its protagonists are a faithful, loving old couple whose spirits inhabit pine trees that are far separated in space; but the husband's spirit travels many miles each night to meet his wife's in happy communion. The pine tree, which is always green and grows to the age of "a thousand years," is another symbol of long life and of

ABOVE:
Three views of Ito in A Pair of Fans
1927

RIGHT:
Ito in Spring Rain
1929.
This photograph by Toyo Miyatake
was hung in the London Salon of Photography
of 1930

OPPOSITE PAGE:
Ito in Impression of a Chinese Actor
Painting by Carl Link

A MACFADDEN PUBLICATION

immortality. In a popular version of this story, the couple, like Ovid's, after a long, happy life died in the same hour and were changed into a tree—a pine—with single trunk and double branches, and when the two spirits emerge in human form on moonlit nights to sweep away the pine needles, they are accompanied by a crane and a tortoise.[22]

Whichever fable we prefer makes no difference; the idea is the same. As in all Ito's dances, there is no pantomime; the idea, directly expressed by conventional gesture, is oneness, seen in the joining of the fans (or of the hands that hold the fans) and in their separate symmetrical movement of travels through life and through eternity. It is the immortal oneness of human love and companionship. Performed without fans, this dance recalls nothing so much as certain figures on ancient Greek vases. Though costume, fan, and fable be regarded as Japanese, the idea is neither of the East nor of the West; it is merely universal.

Ito did compose a number of dances in avowed ancient Greek style. For example, *Gnossiennes I* and *II* (interpretations of Satie's music) are reminiscent of Minoan and archaic Greek art. *Gnossienne I* recalls the gaudy dances, processions, banqueting, and other convivialities that enliven Etruscan tomb paintings—the spirit of life lived well on earth in contrast to a dank hereafter in the tomb; *Gnossienne II*, Cretan religious celebration, also pretty much of this world.

Greek Warrior, an interpretation of a Schumann étude, expresses the joy of combat, as a warrior from an ancient vase fights his invisible enemy with an imaginary spear, on foot or mounted on an invisible steed, and finally clashes his invisible weapon against his invisible shield in ringing triumph.

Tragedy is also done to a Schumann étude and it too suggests the mind of Greece through its strong, angular movement, definite counterpoint, and tightly controlled muscular intensity. Like Yamada *Tone Poem II*, it is a choreographic outcry against life's injustices, with alternate appeals to, and defiance of, all the powers on earth, in heaven, and in man's own soul. Unlike the *Tone Poem,* however, *Tragedy* does not end on a note of defiant menace; it is a struggle ending in downfall. It could be Macbeth's terrible life after the murder, or Lear's stormy battles. It could be Antigone's high courage and stubborn acts for family and the gods that watch over the dead. It could be Oedipus engaging his destiny with the single weapon, human intelligence. The viewing of those tragic struggles does not plunge the spectator in gloom. Rather he is exhilarated by the hero's or heroine's greatness of action and feels a thrill of pride at belonging to the same race. So it is with this dance of Ito's.

The mood of *Lotus Land* is as vague and dreamy as that of Homer's land of lotus-eaters, which is thought not to have existed on earth but only in men's minds. The rhythm of sea and wind which underscores the music's melody runs through the dance, as it does through Homer's verse. And Ito's first welcoming gestures seem to recall the seductive hospitality and gracious life offered by the gentle inhabitants to Odysseus' brute sailormen. If so, Homer's land was in the East, over Indochina way. And who knows if it was not? Odysseus' ships were blown for nine days before a strange wind that swept them out of this world into the unknown.[23] These welcoming gestures suggest Apsaras, not the heavenly courtesans who danced for the pleasure of sensual Hindu gods, but those other Apsaras that serve as angels and call men to love of the divinity as they fly aloft with chastely bended knee and elbow—Buddha's Apsaras.[24] For wherever else we are, we are in the land of the true lotus, symbol of heavenly purity unsullied by the world's slime out of which it grows like a soul aspiring from its muddy passions, symbol of spiritual enlightenment in the unfolding petals, symbol of the all-present future-present-past with bud, flower, and seed together on the same plant.[25] It is a land where Buddha conquers the temptations of the flesh, repulses evil in all its forms, sows good abroad in the world, sets rolling the wheel of truth and righteousness, preaches with energy, and attains perfect enlightenment. Above all, it is a land where we behold the calm, reflective Buddha seated upon the lotus, symbol of "purity of the spirit that will endure beyond experience."[26] Such are the dance's fable and idea, flowing from the music itself.

In a certain sense *White Peacock* is akin to *Lotus Land*, but it is more simple, less complex, both in fable and in idea. *Lotus Land*, to be sure, leaves us with a single image, the contemplative Buddha, which "lays a spell upon the mind, woos it from the restless world, and draws it inward to the divine ecstasy of absolute contemplation."[27] As a whole, however, *Lotus Land* is made up of variegated allusions that merge harmoniously into this final effect. Like *White Peacock*, it has an all-enveloping mood but it is one that now conceals, now reveals, its essence. *White Peacock*, on the contrary, directly proclaims the magnificence of nature, the sense of life and the power of life, not only in man but in all living things. The idea penetrates our consciousness in the form of an overwhelming but only half-defined emotion.

Ito and Charles Griffes, the composer of the music, were friends. During the last three years of Griffes' life they were associated in theatrical ventures in which Griffes performed his own compositions, so that Ito must have heard him play the piano version of "The White Peacock" a good many times. But the idea for the dance as we know it seems to have come to him later. He awoke early one morning, he said, and, in that state where sleep and dream are not yet quite gone, saw "whiteness" to the remembered sound of Griffes' music. Just so, the dance conjures up an infinite whiteness which our thought—our emotion at least—inhabits without effort, for it is an infinity within our own psyche. William Butler Yeats wrote of Ito: "He was able, as he rose from the floor where he had been sitting cross-legged, or as he threw out an arm, to recede from us into some more powerful life . . . he receded but to inhabit as it were the deeps of the mind."[28] By the same path, this dance finds its way unerringly into our inmost thought. Although sharp step, feathery hands, and sweeping wing bear traces of the bird's charac-teristic movement, rhythmic restraint renders these gestures formal and of a godlike dignity and grandeur, so as to suggest such flight as no peacock ever knew. The beautiful birdlike creature is a manifestation of the eternal in all its creatures: pure beauty, pure love, pure life caught in a momentary vision of delicately flashing white. Yet throughout the dance there is a pervasive tenderness and a sense of brotherhood in all life, reminding us that we too have a part in nature's scheme.

This same affinity between the human spirit and external nature permeates the remaining dance poems of my catalogue. The merry spirals of *Ladybug* and the carefree mothlike movements of *Joy* suggest life's brief beauty, as it were, in the flight of an insect. *Chopin Étude* has a joyous mood but it is one that is more intense, even bordering on the savage. Franz Liszt wrote that Chopin "made forays into the world of dryads, oreads, and nymphs of spring and ocean."[29] He should have included another class of Greek spirit, a wilder one, the maenads, female followers of the nature-god Dionysus, who held their nightly revels in the darkness of pine woods on mountain heights. These are the spirits of *Étude*, the mysterious, frightening element in nature.[30]

ABOVE: *Dancing figure*   *Chopin Étude*
Drawing by Michio Ito

ABOVE RIGHT:
Poster for recital Imperial Theatre   Tokyo   1931

With the Debussy interpretations, *Golliwogg's Cakewalk, Little Shepherdess, Maid with the Flaxen Hair*, and *Arabesque II*, we come to a sunny nature, a so-to-speak French, civilized nature, more human than external and yet close to mother earth.

Ito's Golliwogg, as in the Upton tales,[31] initially appears out of the mysterious night, a powerful "gnome with flying hair" but also "a jolly dog" with an "artist's head," "kind face," and "kindly smile." That is, he is a gentleman, nature's gentleman. He is a knight-errant, with more sense perhaps than Don Quixote but no less ridiculous, who comes to the rescue of some silly, inconsiderate maidens (really bald-headed wooden dolls) and engages with them in ill-advised adventures out in the topsy-turvy world of men. He is a true gentleman, who, like Don Quixote, is never quite put out by the indignities of fortune. Between visits to the North Pole, the circus, the seaside, et cetera, he attends the young ladies to the ballroom,[32] where he astonishes the assemblage with his elegant presence as he glides high and jumps wide, minces it exquisitely, and even displays a nonchalant foot in ragtime clog. Neither music nor dance relates the Upton adventures; they only suggest the idea, that is, the Golliwogg in us all. As this gnome appeared suddenly out of the darkness, so, in music and dance, he finally jumps back into the pond, or into the void or some unknown abyss of the mind.

Little Shepherdess is also close to the soil. Her littleness makes great the nature around her. She wakes to the countryside's early morning sounds, drives her flock, rests in the warmth of noon, rescues a strayed lamb, plays with her dog, dances heys over the sheep as evening comes on, and finally gazes over their woolly backs into the dim light beyond. She appears to be a real shepherdess with her real shepherd's crook. Her gestures even approach pantomime, but they are not pantomime; through their harmonious design they take on an ethereal cast. She is such a perfect shepherdess, so rhythmically blended with her flock and with the air and sun and valleys, that she wins a kind of permanence in our thoughts and is there transformed into pure spirit. Her gestures all become symbols of protective love and of the contentment that comes from loving; she is the idea "shepherd" and all her gestures are metaphors of that idea. Her costume makes us think of David and his "green pastures," for her hair is a sunny yellow, her velvet tunic bright green, and her long skirt of light-brown earth color flowered over with bright blossoms.

The "maid with the flaxen hair" frolics in the sun but unlike the "shepherdess" is an idle girl, a lily of the field, showing off her shining beauty with somewhat the same innocent vanity as the "faun," and like him with a certain whimsicality of movement. But she is not an elemental part of ourselves as he was; she is a passing fancy, a thing of air and evanescence, a sunbeam set to music.

LEFT: *Poster with figure from Debussy Arabesque II*
Los Angeles   1935   Drawing by Michio Ito

RIGHT: Debussy Arabesque II *second and third figures*
Sketch by Michio Ito

Bumptious vanity brought low by a banana peel has ever been a source of comedy. When equated with "sex" it is perhaps funniest of all. Surely pure sex uncomplicated by other passions has no business in art if it is not comic business. It is this kind of sex that rears its silly head in *Arabesque II,* and quite appropriately this dance is pure comedy, one with no deeper idea than that sex is comic. Three dancers are involved. A lover in love with love and all the girls, when mocked by the capricious objects of his affections (two in number), finds instant consolation by slowly catapulting himself heels over head into a parlous state of extreme relaxation.

There are touches of comedy or lightness, as I have indicated, in many of Ito's dance poems, but usually the idea is serious in nature. This does not mean that any one of the dances is sad or depressing. Although the idea strike a deeper chord within us, it is always one that thrills, that leaves us with a feeling of joy. Even in the more dramatic poems, such as *Tragedy* and the Yamada *Tone Poems I* and *II,* the spirit is lifted; we are exhilarated not only visually but also, as it were, by a kinesthetic participation in a valiant human struggle. Plato derived the Greek word for dance (*chorós*) from the word for joy (*chará*).[33] His etymology is not necessarily accurate but it may indicate a quality in the dancing of his day, in particular of the dances performed as part of the tragedies. Poets have frequently stressed joy as the end or purpose of *their* creations. Dylan Thomas said, "All that matters about poetry is your enjoyment of it."[34] Present-day critics concur in this opinion and extend it to include all art. Anthony Burgess writes that part of the blessedness of art "lies in its being conceived in joy";[35] and Helen Gardner, "People think of pleasure as a low word, but all art exists to give pleasure."[36] Poets, as well as critics, who have undertaken to discover the source of this joy or pleasure have come up with pretty much the same answer: in Wordsworth's words, "the pleasure which the mind derives from the perception of similitude in dissimilitude."[37] Yeats puts it a slightly different way: "The end of art is the ecstasy awakened by the presence before an ever-changing mind of what is permanent in the world," and conversely, "All art is the disengaging of a soul from place and history."[38] Laurence Binyon is more explicit. In explaining the canons of Chinese painting he wrote: "The artist must pierce beneath the mere aspect of the world to seize and himself to be possessed by that great cosmic rhythm of the spirit which sets the currents of life in motion. We should say in Europe that he must seize the universal in the particular."[39] In Western art, he says, where the emphasis has been on man, there has always been an opposition between man and the rest of nature but in the East no such barrier exists. "The continuity of the universe, the perpetual stream of change through its matter, are accepted as things of Nature, felt in the heart and not merely learnt as the conclusions of delving science."[40] "The winds of the air have become his desires and the clouds his wandering thoughts. . . . The universe, in its wholeness and freedom, has become his spiritual home."[41] Or, as Binyon sums it up, art at once "satisfies our instinct for order and our instinct for freedom."[42] That is, art tells us we are individuals but essential parts of an orderly universe. In the words of Anthony Burgess, "We go to art for the *illusion* of order and this gives us a euphoria with no morning-after of shame or hang-over."[43]

Ito sought this "illusion of order" but never the illusion of a reality of the senses. In pursuit of the illusion of order, he consciously (as he often stated) sought to combine the art of East and West, emphasizing man's suffering and joy but always in relation to controlling powers of the universe, as we have seen to be so evident, for example, in *Ball, Yamada Tone Poems I* and *II,* and *White Peacock.* Nature in its manifold aspects, the universe as a whole, is present in Ito's dance poems. Against the backdrop of nature, and merging with it, moves some human concept in visible shape. As we have seen in the dances described, it is often individual man himself, curious, eager, frightened in the presence of Nature—whether within or without himself—defying her, compromising with her, loving her, adoring her, surrendering self to his adoration, but never going down to abject defeat before her. Specifically, in none of Ito's creations does the dancer wallow on the floor or on other pieces of furniture. The spirit is never destroyed; the sensuous, the material, never takes over. As Ito often remarked, "Art gives a spiritual interpretation to the visible, and material signification to the invisible; the artist *must* make these two relations manifest." Here we return to his insistence on the "idea" as essential to artistic creation. Ito's dances are never pure fable, that is, a series of exciting events with no further meaning. The fable is uniformly simple (as Yeats counseled) and more often than not absorbed in the idea, which is expressed directly in formal, symbolic

27

movement. For "material signification" does not mean actual representation. Realistic gesture has no part in these dances. Even in the comic *Arabesque II* the few bits of pantomime have been stylized almost out of existence.

Ito recognized the instinctive or natural gesture as the base of dancing, but for artistic dance he felt that realistic gesture, whether instinctive, deictic, or imitative, was to be formalized in order to serve the idea. Not only does it have to be subjected to rhythm, temporal and spatial; it must also take on symbolic meaning. "Just as in language, we use concrete images out of context to express larger, more intense, more abstract conceptions, so the dancer uses the stylized form of what was once a purely imitative gesture to suggest a more poetic or grander idea. . . . Consider the metaphoric use of a word, the verb *sow*. Literally we sow seeds in the ground; metaphorically we sow wild oats, dissension, destruction, the wind, and so on. It is the same with the ancient gesture of sowing in which grain is taken, say, by the right hand from a vessel held on the left shoulder and thrown in a wide arc over the head and into the ground on the right side of the sower."[44] This gesture, in stylized form, is used in the Scriabin *Prelude IX,* for the idea of that dance is Siva, "the sower par excellence, of plants, men, hurricane, fire, war, peace, et cetera—god of creation and destruction."[45] To illustrate with another metaphor common to both language and dance, there is the verb *open* and there is the gesture of opening a door or putting aside a curtain as found in *Prelude V,* where this gesture opens the heart to love, the mind to knowledge, and reveals the godhead and the secrets of the universe. The idea of Ito's dances "is for the most part conveyed by such 'metaphoric' gestures. And their rhythmic arrangement strikes common chords of instinct and of culture in the spectator."[46] Even the traditionally conventional symbols drawn from Eastern dance and art seep easily into our consciousness: for example, the fire signature in *Prelude IX,* the use of the Japanese fan to suggest a sword being drawn from its scabbard, or of the pair of fans to suggest the butterfly that symbolizes immortality. Most of the conventional gestures used by Ito, however, are reminiscent of Western painting and sculpture: for example, the ancient gesture of rejoicing with upraised arms bent at elbow so familiar from Christian art that we can scarcely tell whether it is a conventional gesture or an instinctive one that has undergone an artistic sea change.

In one sense, Ito's technique was simple, or proceeded from a simple base. Theoretically at least, his dances were composed of ten gestures—gestures of the arms. Like the ancient Greeks, he believed that the upper body, especially in movement of arms and head, was the medium through which an idea could best be made visible, buttocks, legs, and feet being feeble instruments for this purpose and able to perform only an ancillary function in the body's movement. These ten arm gestures, which he likened to the twelve notes on the piano and their manifold combinations in musical composition,[47] Ito used with such variation of plane, angle to body, position of hands, context, and rhythm that his dances present seemingly endless variety.

Of the thirty-seven dance poems described in the above catalogue, no two open with the same gesture, or series of gestures; and this is true of all other dances of Ito's with which I am familiar. No dance ends with the gesture with which it begins. Initial gestures are different from one another because the idea of each dance is introduced immediately and the idea is in each case different, although the general theme running through all the dances is the same: love in its many manifestations. In no dance is the last gesture or phrase a repetition of the opening one, because, like MacLeish's "poem," Ito's dance poem "is not the perfected expression of a predetermined thought but is itself the process of its thinking moving from perception to perception, sense to sense." And, as I have tried to show, none of the dances ends with its final gesture; each continues on in the imagination of the spectator. There is only one apparent exception to this rule, namely, *White Peacock.* Although the final gestures of *White Peacock* do not repeat those of its beginning, the dancer does return with the final phrase to the passive pose assumed before the opening gesture, something that is not true of the other dances. *White Peacock* is somewhat different in nature, or at least in degree, from the other dances. It is highly abstract; line and movement absorb, almost obliterate, symbolic gesture. As within the other dances, there are splendid shifts of emotion; but there is not the same orderly progression of emotion or idea. Rather, before our eyes, but almost without our being aware of it, the idea unfolds in its entirety. The dance is a kind of epiphany, a radiance that vanishes from our sight as imperceptibly as it appeared; but it vanishes into us, where it continues to glow and vibrate before our inner eye. The dancer in that final pose, as in the pose before the dance's beginning, is something outside us, a husk, and of no importance.

Some of Ito's "ten gestures" as used in dance sequences
Sketches by Michio Ito

R/L   I 1A   II 3A/10A   III 10A/3A   IV 2A/6A   V 10B/3A   VI 2A

                           VII 4A   VIII 5A/2A   IX 5A/10B   X10A

ABOVE: Michio Ito   1925   Gestures 4B/5B

OPPOSITE PAGE: Michio Ito   1936
Gestures 4B/7B   Photograph by Toyo Miyatake

I have scarcely mentioned costume, but it too was an essential part of Ito's technique. For the dances with a traditional flavor—*Tango, Minuet, Javanese*—he used traditional costume. For dances more removed from time and place, the costume was more suggestive of the idea perhaps than of the fable. In all instances, Ito composed with a view to the costume's enhancing the dance's movement and lending mood to both fable and idea, but always through subtle suggestion of line and color, never through pageantry or parading of garments or other exaggerated effects.

In the same way, Ito avoided spectacle[48] and meretricious display in the dance's composition proper and relied upon suggestion rather than elaboration, believing that an idea, including emotion, exerts more power on the imagination when not completely revealed. Even in his use of metaphor there is no fixed or rigid symbolism, but rather a fine network of subtle associations that link the spectator's thoughts with those of other human beings and draw him out of himself into the life of the dance. None of this allusion is subjective. Both fable and idea are objective, with fable drawn from tradition, and idea from the thoughts and emotions common to many. For most of us at least, the human experience has been illuminated and transformed by the great imaginations of literature, philosophy, and other arts. Our minds are not tabulae rasae; we all have memories, of artistic as well as of actual experiences. It is this common culture and experience that Ito drew upon for idea and for its visible embodiment. Hence the excellences of his style will strike responsive chords in almost all spectators. Outstanding among those excellences are: the strong, incisive gesture; the symmetry of continuous movement and its melding with music; the strength and beauty of line for which Japanese art is noted; the power of suggesting space, atmosphere, and distance by swift, forcible strokes; the economy and simplicity with which he attains emotional effect; the subtle allusion; the satisfying dignity and formality; the buoyancy, lyricism, feeling of joy and freedom; and the tenderness betokening brotherhood, which, like Dylan Thomas's "poem," "makes you know that you are alone and not alone in the unknown world, that your bliss and suffering are forever shared and forever all your own."[49]

Of course, not all this wealth of beauty is accessible to everyone. In Laurence Binyon's words, "Masterpieces are great distinguishers of persons; they will yield all they have to some, while to others they are mute."[50] Ito's dance poems take perfect life in the beholder's mind, not on the stage. The spectator must bring something of himself; his mind must be prepared to enter the dance and complete it. As Duke Ellington sums it up in writing of his own art, the "audience is the other side of the realm that serves the same muse I do."[51]

II "At the Hawk's Well"[1]

Although it was in the alien soil of America that Ito's genius took root and grew to exuberance, it was in England that he made his debut as a professional dancer.[2] The *Times* of Wednesday, 5 May 1915, carried this advertisement for the Coliseum theater, London's great variety house:[3] "Next week . . . Michio Itow the wonderful Japanese male dancer." The same bill was to include the "retired" ballet dancer Adeline Genée and—a matter of curiosity to us today—Miss May Whitty in a one-act comedy. On Monday, 10 May, and for two weeks following, the Coliseum advertisement headlined THE FAMOUS MALE DANCER MICHIO ITOW WHO HAS CREATED A FURORE IN SOCIETY WITH HIS REPERTOIRE OF HARMONIZED EUROPO-JAPANESE DANCES. On Tuesday May 11 there was a brief review, which read in part: "Yesterday there appeared for the first time in a regular bill, the Japanese dancer Mr. Michio Itow, who has studied his art both in East and West, and has constructed a style of dancing which attempts to combine the two ideas. His dances are very short but very novel and impressive."[4]

From these notices, it would seem, Ito already possessed in essence a distinctive style that combined a traditional form of Japanese dance with the new Occidental dance, a style remarkable for economy and strength. How did it come about? Why do we find this young dancer suddenly breaking into prominence on the London stage in May of 1915? Partly from the fortunes of war.

In 1911, at the age of eighteen,[5] with his father's blessing and support, Ito left Tokyo to study singing in Paris. He had studied piano from an early age, and also voice. Indeed, his first appearance on the professional stage was in a German opera, *Buddha,* with Tamaki Miura, at the Imperial Theater, Tokyo, in that same year.[6] In Paris he became disenchanted with opera, and when he saw Nijinsky dance at the Chatelet theater,[7] his ambition began to take a new turn.

Meanwhile, he pondered the nature of art with a capital A. His newly acquired friends, Rodin and Debussy, explained their way of looking at the matter but, as he later said, he "did not understand" them. He spent many hours in the Egyptian rooms of the Louvre, where he became so enamored of Egyptian art that he went to Alexandria, hoping to find there a more complete revelation of its secret. Again he was disappointed. He found nothing in Alexandria to compare with the collection at the Louvre. But he did find an old Egyptian man, barefoot and in rags, but learned, who endeavored to explain to him the principles of life and art through the balance at the heart of Egyptian civilization and culture. They spoke to each other in French. Ito remained under this old man's tutelage for some months.

He did not return to Paris, but went to Berlin, where his sister's husband was attached to the Japanese embassy. There, in company with the composer Kōsaku Yamada and the actor Kaoru Osanai, he happened to attend a performance by Isadora Duncan, and his interest in dancing increased. He arranged with Isadora to return to Paris and study with her sister Elizabeth. His brother-in-law, however, persuaded him to remain in Germany and take up the study of the German language instead, perhaps with a view to his entering upon a diplomatic career. It was not for long. While studying German at Leipzig, Ito happened upon an advertisement for the Dalcroze school of eurythmics, a system of education based on rhythm, primarily bodily rhythm, and employing music as its medium—a system with particular application to the arts of music, dancing, and drama.[8]

In Japan, Ito had not only studied piano and European-style singing; he had also had early training in Kabuki, a traditional form of Japanese drama which includes dancing and singing.[9] The Dalcroze system, combining as it did dance, music, and drama, had a kind of affinity with Kabuki. It also appealed to Ito's love of music and to his newly acquired

38

interest in the dance of the Western world, especially as exemplified in Isadora Duncan. He left Leipzig and enrolled as a student at the Dalcroze institute in Hellerau, just outside Dresden. It was the year 1912.

When the war broke out in 1914, Ito found it expedient to leave Germany. In company with three other Japanese[10] he escaped to Holland and from there to England and London. As he spoke no English, he frequented the Café Royal, where his German and French could be understood not only by waiters but also by a good part of the clientele, for the place was a haunt of artists, many of them educated, or at least traveled, on the Continent. In this restaurant Ito found new friends, among them Augustus John, Jacob Epstein, Ezra Pound, and his own compatriots, Tsuguharu Foujita[11] and Kanai Yamamoto,[12] both of whom had been studying painting in France.

Meanwhile, Michio's father had written that, as it was no longer possible for him to continue his studies in Europe, he might as well return to Japan. Michio replied that he wished to remain but that his father need no longer support him, he would make his own way (although he had not the remotest idea how this was to be accomplished). It took him about three weeks to spend his last remittance in a round of "parties."[13] He then consulted his friend Augustus John as to a way of making some money. John promptly introduced him to the glorious amenities of the pawnshop, which Ito found a delightful institution. As he later recalled, he "was surprised that such a convenience existed in this world."

For a time life went on as before, but at last Ito found himself reduced to one old suit (made in Japan), twenty neckties (of German and British make), an empty stomach, an unheated apartment and no money to turn the gas on. He pawned the neckties for sixpence, bought a small loaf of bread for four pennies, inserted the remaining two in the gasometer, mixed the bread with hot water, salt, and pepper, thus making "bread soup," and went to bed to keep warm and ponder the difficulties of his situation.

On evenings when he returned late from the Café Royal, he had noticed street sweepers at work outside his flat. *There* was a job he could do, requiring little knowledge of English and causing him no embarrassment, since the hours were such that his friends would never know of it. With the aid of a dictionary he worked out the phrase, "Where should I go to get that job?" To be doubly sure of being understood, he wrote it on a piece of paper to show the workmen, and then waited for the hour when they would come on their nightly round.

In the meantime an artist friend, one of his Café Royal acquaintance, came by to invite him to a party at the home of Lady Ottoline Morrell, whom the friend referred to as an art patron.[14] He had spoken to her about Ito's dancing. "I can't go," Ito told him; "I have an important business appointment tonight." He was also reluctant to go in his old suit with a black silk handkerchief serving as necktie, no overcoat, no hat; and he was wobbly from inanition, for, aside from the bread soup, he had not eaten for three days. The friend insisted, and when they arrived at Lady Ottoline's she countered Ito's objections of no costume and no music. Henry Wood[15] was to accompany him on the piano and could play whatever music Ito wished, and there was a room full of costumes. Ito did not mention his wobbly muscles. "The costumes she showed me," he later related, "were wonderful—everything real. They made me want to dance. I chose a pair of Turkish trousers and a short Spanish jacket and performed, to some Chopin, a dance I had composed for my examination in Dalcroze."

There were present at this gathering, besides artists such as William Butler Yeats, T. Sturge Moore, and G. B. Shaw,[16] that indefatigable patron of artists Lady Emerald Cunard,[17] who invited Ito to dine at her house the next evening. (He was very glad to accept anything in the way of a dinner invitation.) He was to borrow a costume and after dinner they would go to a party at the home of a friend of hers where he would dance for a larger audience. Lady Cunard told him not to worry, just to dance as he had that evening; he would have the same accompanist, Henry Wood.

About a hundred people were present at this second party. After Ito finished his dance, he was asked to dance again, and yet again. Each time he did, as he put it, "the same stuff" because he did not have any other dance in his repertory. Asked to perform again, he thought it would be a little too much to do the same dance a fourth time, and called out, "I'm tired!" Everyone laughed and said, "Let him stop." (It is interesting to observe that, even in the beginning, Michio Ito did not perform extempore or engage in a "happening," or go in for "self-expression." He was willing to perform only a finished work that he had composed with care.)

40

At supper he was seated near a distinguished-looking man with white hair who tried to engage him in a conversation on Japanese art. Ito begged to be excused because of his lack of English; it would be different if they could converse in German. The gentleman laughed and said, "Let us forget the war." And they talked together in German for a couple of hours.

In a day or two Ito received a letter of thanks which not only expressed admiration and gratitude but also contained a banknote and the following words: "I pray for your success with this £20." The letter was from Herbert Asquith, England's prime minister. It was at his house, at his party, that Ito had danced, and he was the white-haired gentleman with whom Ito had chatted in German.

This whole portion of Michio Ito's life was condensed by Ezra Pound into three lines:

> So Miscio sat in the dark lacking the gasometer penny
> but then said: "Do you speak German?"
> To Asquith in 1914 . . .[18]

With the £20 Ito retrieved his clothes. And, as a result of his dancing, he was taken up by London society; he performed at benefits in theaters, in the homes of the wealthy, and before royalty. Although he said his "Dalcroze" interpretation of Chopin was the only dance in his repertoire at the time of the Asquith party, he must have played with ideas for dance interpretations before then. We know, for example, that in Paris in 1911 he frequently danced for Debussy's little daughter while Debussy accompanied him at the piano.[19] Certainly during the months following the Asquith party he would have composed a number of dances for his many appearances.[20]

From Lady Ottoline Morrell's memoirs it appears that Ito went frequently to the Thursday evenings she and her husband Philip held at their London house from November 1914 to April 1915. At these evenings, dancing, much of it impromptu, was the main diversion. In Lady Ottoline's words,

> Those who came often dressed themselves up in gay Persian, Turkish, and other oriental clothes, of which I had a store. Philip played tunes of all kinds on the pianola, a new toy—Brahms . . .

Mozart, or even some of the good old music-hall song tunes—such as, "Watch your step" or "Get out and get under" and "Dixie." . . . [She then describes the guests.] There was Guevara, a painter who was always called Chile, who brought a wonderful Japanese dancer, Ito. Ito had a long, dark, antique type of face like a monk, and as he danced, his movements were marvelously beautiful. I shall never forget the dance that he invented to "Yip i Yaddy i Yay." He would ask Philip to play a tune through, then think about it for a few minutes, and then start his interpretation of it, wild and imaginative, with intense passion and form.[21]

Again, we see, Ito did not dance as the spirit moved him but, even in those informal gatherings, attempted to compose an artistically true interpretation of the music. And, judging from what we know of his later habits of composition, it is fair to assume that he "thought about" the music and his interpretation, not just for "a few minutes" but for a longer time and, no doubt, when he was away from the Morrells'.

That he worked hard over the dances he was performing at private parties and public benefits and also over those for the Coliseum appearance is certain. We have his account of the way he perfected one of these dances, his *Fox*. This account also illustrates the importance he assigned to idea and to meditation: "My fox dance is furtive and independent and cunning and staccato. I studied a fox and his ways with a biscuit long before I worked out my dance. Then I went to a great hill in Hampstead and I made my soul into the soul of a fox, and so I evolved my fox dance."[22] Donn Byrne, in a chapter on the mystic beliefs and ritual surrounding the fox, has testified to the power of this dance of Michio Ito's.[23]

After the Coliseum engagement, Ito was offered contracts to perform at theaters in other English cities but he was prevented from accepting because of an injury suffered in an accident. As part of his convalescence, Lady Ottoline suggested he take a rest at her place near Oxford.[24]

When he came back to London and the Café Royal, he learned that Ezra Pound had been inquiring for him. Pound wanted Ito to help him with the editing of Ernest Fenollosa's manuscripts.[25] In 1913 Fenollosa's widow had given Pound her husband's manuscripts, which included translations of Noh plays and information about their history and performance.[26] Pound was to make poetic translations of the plays and edit

Ito in his Fox Dance
1915
Photograph by
Alvin Langdon Coburn

43

the other notes. When he asked Ito for his help, Ito's response was, "Noh is the damnedest thing in this world." Pound replied, "I am only an American. You say Noh is the damnedest thing in this world—which means you know more about it than I do. That is why you have to help me."[27]

A little more than a year before Ito entered the Pound-Fenollosa picture, Ezra Pound had read William Butler Yeats some of the translations.[28] In Pound's words, "W. B. Yeats was at once kindled by the imperfect versions of Noh which I was able to make from Fenollosa's notes. He started writing plays in Noh form for his Irish theater and for performances where no western stage was available."[29]

It was Noh that gave Yeats's dramatic work a new direction;[30] and he "invented," as he said, the play for dancers.[31] The first of these, *At the Hawk's Well,* in which both Pound and Ito had a hand,[32] was composed in 1915-16. Yeats told Ito, at the time, that he had come to dislike the theater—all theater—and had determined to write no more plays.[33] After hearing some of the Fenollosa translations, however, he was encouraged to return to playwriting, but in a new style based on Noh. Hence when Ezra Pound asked for Ito's help with his Noh book (apparently in the early summer of 1915) William Butler Yeats was no less interested than Ezra Pound.[34]

It happened that there were in London at the time two artists—painters—who had been classmates of Ito's at high school in Tokyo. These two men, Tami Kume and Jisoīchi Kayano, were versed in *utai,* the singing part of the Noh play. Ito took them to Pound's flat in order that Yeats and Pound might hear them perform this art.[35] Twenty-four years later Pound extolled the Noh singing in no uncertain terms,[36] but when he first heard it he was "not interested in it." Ito said, "I told you so!"[37]

The effect on Michio Ito, however, and presumably on Yeats, was quite different. Ito later said that he suddenly recognized the beauty of *utai* when he heard it in Pound's flat, and that he understood Noh for the first time when he saw Fenollosa's manuscripts there in London and recalled what Gordon Craig had said about the use of the mask: that a mask made by an artist portrays the soul of the character as conceived by the poet.[38] The mask, Craig had written, carries conviction because the artist limits the statement he places upon it. "The face of the actor carries no such conviction; it is over-full of fleeting expression—frail, restless, and disturbing."[39] Ito perceived that the effect achieved by the Noh mask was the same as that desired by Gordon Craig.

There is no record of the impression produced on Yeats by the *utai;* but, from the assimilation of Noh in *At the Hawk's Well*, it may be assumed that it made a greater impression on him than on Pound. Ezra Pound sometimes made fun of Yeats's musical sense, implying, for example, that Yeats did not "know a fugue from a frog."[40] Yet it seems certain that he, Pound, did not immediately appreciate this Japanese form of singing, although Yeats apparently did, for the *Hawk's Well* became a "Noh" play and Ito was persuaded to take one of the roles and set the movements of the other players.[41]

Ito later said he had not seen a Noh play since the age of seven, and then only under compulsion.[42] In order to help Pound with the Fenollosa notes he had to study the archaic Japanese in which the plays and much of the commentary are written. When it came to performing in Yeats's play and directing the other players' movement and gesture, however, he could not have been at a complete loss; he was not entirely unfamiliar with the Noh form and feeling and even the Noh technique. As noted above, he had studied Kabuki, which is based on Noh, with plots, music, and dance borrowed from the Noh theater, although most of the elements had been vulgarized; and, of course, a stylized, often exaggerated, makeup in Kabuki replaces the simple, natural though idealized, mask and masklike immobile unpainted face characteristic of Noh.[43] It is interesting to note that although the other two actors in the play (the Old Man and the Young Man) wore masks as in a Noh play, Ito, as Guardian of the Well, wore only a kind of partial mask, or rather his headdress covered the sides of his face, and the rest was painted much in Kabuki style to resemble a mask. The chorus likewise had their faces painted in exaggerated style to give the appearance of masks.[44]

The dance performed by the hawklike Guardian, as composed by Michio Ito, was, in fact, a modified Noh dance—tense, continuous movement with suble variations on its monotony, inducing a trancelike state in both personages and audience—but its increase in tempo was more rapid than in genuine Noh and the arm movement was broad and smoothly dramatic, recalling Egyptian representations of the hawk with spread wings and giving a feeling of a great bird's gliding and wheeling.[45]

RIGHT ABOVE:
Ito as Guardian of the Well
At the Hawk's Well   London   1916
Drawing by Edmund Dulac

RIGHT BELOW:
Old Man
At the Hawk's Well
London   1916
Design by Edmund Dulac
Showing Egyptian influence

OPPOSITE PAGE:
At the Hawk's Well   London   1916
Ito wearing hawk headdress
designed and made by Dulac and Ito
Photograph by Alvin Langdon Coburn

46

The gesture of the other two actors and of the chorus was also stylized in the ancient Egyptian manner and of course was done to the rhythm of the verse. Indeed, the Old Man's pose in the Dulac costume sketch, with the hand at the knee, is the ancient Egyptian gesture of greeting described by Herodotus, a gesture retained in Egyptian Muslim worship today.[46] Is this sketch Michio Ito's old man of Cairo? Dulac's design for the Hawk's costume and headdress, as Ito himself remarked, was Egyptian, and Ito was pleased with it; but he was not pleased with the Young Man's mask, for he felt it smacked of the *Arabian Nights* which Dulac had been illustrating.[47] Egyptian art had a strong influence on Ito. In later dance compositions he took for his own the balance, the rhythmic vigor and energy of figures carved on Egyptian monuments, most notably in his interpretations of Schumann, Yamada, and Scriabin.

Another link between Egypt and the *Hawk's Well* may be seen in the subtitle; the play was first performed and published under the title *At the Hawk's Well or The Waters of Immortality*.[48] The hawk in ancient Egypt symbolized the celestial principle, representing not only the sun-god Horus but also Osiris "the guarantor of *immortality*."[49]

Ito, it is said, worked out the dance movement and taught it to Yeats.[50] Pound as well as Ito worked on the production.[51] Edmund Dulac designed and made the masks and costumes and composed the music.[52] Curtis B. Bradford, who studied seven versions of the play—five manuscripts in Yeats's hand and two typescripts—shows that, as rehearsals progressed and Yeats became increasingly aware of the excellence of Ito's dance interpretation, he cut certain songs and speeches as unnecessary and relied on dance alone to convey the meaning expressed in those passages.[53] We also know that as rehearsals progressed Yeats became more and more enthusiastic about this play as a form of drama he could pursue in the future. On 26 March, a week before the performance, he wrote to Lady Gregory, "I believe I have at last found a dramatic form that suits me." But he was far from satisifed with the performance of the musician, who was a professional, and with Henry Ainley, a professional actor who played "the young man." In the same letter he wrote: "The play goes on well except for Ainley, who waves his arms like a drowning kitten, and the musician, who is in a constant rage."[54] Ezra Pound (in the canto quoted above) recorded Ito's comment that even behind the mask Ainley's face was constantly working and grimacing.[55]

48

On the whole, however, Yeats was delighted with the two performances of the play.[56] The first, in the nature of a dress rehearsal, was given on 2 April 1916 in Lady Cunard's drawing room before an audience of invited guests.[57] There was no stage lighting and no scenery except, it would seem, a Gordon Craig screen as background. The poetry described the "scenery": the rhythmic cadences of verse, music, and dance supplied the emotional atmosphere; and the masks and masklike faces, "keeping always an appropriate distance from life," seemed "images of those profound emotions that exist only in solitude and silence." There was no theatricality to interfere with the play's own imagery. "Only those who cared for poetry were invited," wrote Yeats, "and the audience and the players and I myself were pleased."[58]

Besides Yeats's perhaps biased view, we have the opinion of a disinterested witness, one of the invited guests, Edward Marsh, Churchill's secretary and unofficially an amateur and patron of the arts. He wrote:

I had to go away in the middle which was wretched, as I was getting quite worked up and impressed. It's the beginning of an attempt to give poetic plays in such an inexpensive way that they can be done for quite small audiences—many of the conventions are taken from the traditional dramas ... of the Japanese nobility. I find I can manage quite well without *any* scenery at all—but they had been a little too careful not to disturb the room and I couldn't help being disconcerted, just when I had persuaded myself that I had before me a wild mountain tract of semi-historic Ireland, to notice the characters skirting round a Louis XV table covered with French novels. The actors wore masks made by Dulac, awfully good, and I found it quite easy to accept the convention.[59]

Two days later the *Hawk's Well* was given a semipublic performance in Lady Islington's big drawing room for the benefit of a charity.[60] It was attended by three hundred fashionable people including Queen Alexandra, which caused Yeats to remark, "My muses were but half welcome."[61] Aside from the nature of the audience and the sanctions it imposed (presumably the tables had been moved back or at least cleared of French novels), the only difference in the second presentation was the addition of a platform for the players; and the play was preceded by a concert arranged and conducted by Thomas Beecham, the director of the Royal London Philharmonic.[62] Although Yeats was not so well satisfied

49

as at the earlier, more intimate presentation, still, even after this second performance, he was jubilant enough to write Lady Gregory, "The form is a discovery and the dancing and masks wonderful."[63]

Another poet was *much* impressed by the play, T. S. Eliot, who later wrote:

> Yeats was well known, of course; but to me, at least, Yeats did not appear, until after 1917 [*read* 1916], to be anything but a minor survivor of the '90's. (After that date, I saw him differently. I remember well the impression of the first performance of *The Hawk's Well,* in a London drawing room, with a celebrated Japanese dancer in the role of the hawk, to which Pound took me. And thereafter one saw Yeats rather as a more eminent contemporary than as an elder from whom one could learn.)[64]

Eliot's opinion has been echoed by a host of Yeats scholars.[65] Yeats himself, at least as far as his plays were concerned, recognized the artistic importance of the step he was taking. During rehearsals of the *Hawk's Well* he wrote: "I have invented a form of drama, distinguished, indirect and symbolic and having no need of mob or press to pay its way—an aristocratic form. . . . I shall hope to write another of the same sort."[66] On the day of the first performance he again wrote of his excitement over the new play, in which masks were being used for the first time in serious drama in the modern world, concluding: "I hope to create a form of drama which may delight the best minds of my time. . . . I shall have a success that would have pleased Sophocles. . . . I shall be happier than Sophocles. I shall be as lucky as a Japanese poet at the Court of the Shogun.[67]

In spite of his satisfaction over the play, Yeats decided to put off more performances until he could get rid of Ainley and the offending musicians.[68] Meantime Michio Ito was offered a contract to appear in a New York theater. Yeats advised him to accept, saying the war had made London an unsatisfactory place for artistic theater and dance. "Why don't you go to America for three years?" he asked Ito. "After three years you can come back to London."[69] In the early autumn of 1916 Michio Ito came to the United States. He never returned to England.

Although Yeats had expressed his intention to write more "plays for dancers,"[70] after Ito's departure he seemed to hesitate for want of dance

"*Even the Japanese
Heel up and weight on toe*"
*W. B. Yeats
Bronze statue of Michio Ito
by Allan Clark
1920*

*"I saw him as the tragic image
that has stirred my imagination"* W. B. Yeats
Photograph of Michio Ito by Toyo Miyatake

52

inspiration, or rather, for want of one particular dancer. He had written at the time of the rehearsals for the *Hawk's Well,* "My play is made possible by a Japanese dancer," and "For some weeks now I have been elaborating my play in London where alone I can find the help I need, Mr. Dulac's mastery of design and Mr. Itow's genius of movement."[71] After Ito had left, Yeats elucidated his hesitation:

> Perhaps I shall turn to something else now that our Japanese dancer, Mr. Itow, whose minute intensity of movement in the dance of the hawk so well suited our small room and private art, has been hired by a New York theatre, or perhaps I shall find another dancer. I am certain, however, that whether I grow tired or not—and one does grow tired of always quarrying the stone for one's statue—I have found out the only way the subtler forms of literature can find dramatic expression.[72]

Even in 1920, after he had composed three more "plays for dancers," Yeats was still troubled about the dancing and its music. In the preface to *Four Plays for Dancers,* he wrote:

> Should I make a serious attempt, which I may not, being rather tired of the theatre, to arrange and supervise performances, the dancing will give me most trouble, for I know but vaguely what I want. I do not want any existing form of stage dancing, but . . . something more reserved, more self-controlled. . . .

> At the end of this book there is some music by Mr. Rummel . . . for "The Dreaming of the Bones." . . . I notice that Mr. Rummel has written no music for the dance, and I have some vague memory that when we talked it over in Paris he felt that he could not without the dancer's help.[73]

Earl Miner expresses the opinion that the difficulty in getting a dancer-choreographer to replace Michio Ito led Yeats in subsequent plays "to substitute patterned movement for dance."[74] Professor Miner also shows how Ito's influence as a dancer and as a Japanese of samurai family reached into Yeats's lyric poetry as well, where one finds the persistent images of dance and dancer and of Japan "as an aristocratic culture."[75] In addition to acknowledging his dependence on Ito for composition of dance and music, and also for performance of the dance, Yeats had

53

already pointed to him as a source of poetic inspiration, saying, "I [saw] him as the tragic image that has stirred my imagination."[76]

Yeats again referred to his debt to Ito in a letter to Quinn, 23 July 1918, in which he asked for news of Ito's production of the *Hawk's Well* in New York. It had been performed on 10 July with Japanese players and with music by the Japanese composer Yamada, without Yeats's consent and somewhat to his chagrin because he supposed it to have been given before the general public. But a hint of his feeling of gratitude to Ito may be found in this statement toward the end of the letter: "Circumstances have arisen which would make it ungracious to forbid Ito to play *The Hawk* as he will."[77] The letter continues: "I had thought to escape the press and people digesting their dinners, and to write for my friends. However, Ito and his Japanese players should be interesting." In spite of what precedes it, that last sentence does perhaps betray an enthusiasm both for *The Hawk* and for Michio Ito, and one wonders if Yeats would not have taken pleasure in any good performance of his play, no matter what the audience.[78]

Ito, for his part, was so impressed by the poetic beauty and dramatic power of *At the Hawk's Well* that he presented it twice in the United States, in New York in 1918 and in California in 1929. In 1939 he translated the play into Japanese for performance in Japan,[79] where it ultimately came to be regarded as a genuine Noh play and was made a part of Japan's permanent Noh repertory.[80] Throughout his career in the United States Ito was constantly searching for a poet who could write verse suited to his form of dance interpretation, but always in vain. Nevertheless, the aesthetic influence he had felt in London—in the company of Yeats and Pound—followed him to the New World. His style, marked by Noh ideals, became more and more a distinctive thing of his own, a happy marriage of old and new, of East and West.

54

III The Artist in New York

In New York Michio Ito did not immediately find an atmosphere congenial to his muse. He was met at the pier by the producer who had hired him to appear in his theater. It soon became apparent that the darling of that artistic gem, *At the Hawk's Well*, was to display his artistry in a musical "sex comedy" about two mate-swapping couples. In brief, he was to dance in front of their two beds! As Ito mildly put it, he "released the producer from his contract."[1] Michio Ito never publicly identified this man but his brother Yuji Ito said it was Ziegfeld. There is more reason to believe it was Oliver Morosco.[2]

Ito was not permitted to remain idle, however, On 13 November 1916 the Washington Square Players presented *Bushido* with Michio Ito as codirector and scene designer. *Bushido* was a Kabuki play given in English at the Comedy Theater, with the French actor José Reuben in the leading role of Pine Tree (Matsuo).[3] Among the players was Katharine Cornell, making her debut as a professional actress. She had one line, of four words, "My son, my son," and it was, she said, a very exciting moment when she was told she could have the part.[4]

Besides his training in Kabuki and his proficiency as dancer and choreographer, Michio Ito had been schooled in the most advanced theory and practice of Western theater: direction, scenic design, and lighting. At Hellerau, in the remarkable playhouse designed by Adolphe

55

Appia and Heinrich Tessenow, he had observed as a participant the joint production of Appia, Dalcroze, and Salzmann.[5] In England, Gordon Craig's theory of masks and use of screens had been realized in *At the Hawk's Well.* Evidently Ito now put observation and experience to good use. *Bushido* was hailed as a bright new triumph for the Washington Square Players:

> Japanese tragedy admirably staged, climax at the Washington Square Players' finest program. (*New York Times,* 14 Nov. 1916, p. 8)

> *Bushido* one of the finest and most successful things the Players have ever done. . . . The beauty and restraint with which it was presented ennobled it so that it is difficult indeed to trace its relationship to the maudlin jingoism that passes for patriotism in the average war play today. (Josephine A. Meyer in *Theatre Arts Magazine* [Dec. 1917], p. 27)

> The thread of a rhythmic continuity may unite any group of actors for the realization of a dramatic piece. Such was the effect—of a remarkable emotional unity—made by the play *Bushido* as produced by the Washington Square Players in 1916. Restraint, formalism, ritual, hiding tender humanity, was the theme of the play, consistently interpreted by the restrained and simple movements of the actors. This play was staged by M. Ito, a Japanese, and a graduate of the Dalcroze school in Hellerau. (Elizabeth S. Allen, "Eurythmics for the Theatre," *Theatre Arts Magazine* [Jan. 1919], p. 45)

> That deeply touching and austerely noble version of the Japanese classic, Bushido, so unforgettably published by the Washington Square Players on their bill at the Comedy Theatre, with its haunting personification of the devoted Matsuo by that accomplished player, Mr. José Reuben. This superb presentment of a masterpiece of drama atones for the profitless trivialities and futilities into which the Washingtonians appear to be declining. (Laurence Gilman in *North American Review* [Jan. 1917], pp. 133-134)

> Best bill seen at the Comedy. Washington Square Players set new mark. *Bushido* . . . is a splendid achievement. In costuming and setting it is remarkable. . . . The altogether admirable set for the play was designed by William Pennington and Michio Itow. The play was

staged under the direction of Itow and Edward Goodman. This is the most difficult piece of business the players have attempted and it is well worth the doing. (Heywood Broun in *New York Tribune*, 14 Nov. 1916, p. 7)

Every once in a blue moon, a playwright or a player achieves a moment of dramatic suspense so intense that the theatre grows still as death and your heart stops beating. Such a moment is the climax of *Bushido*, itself the climax of the most successful program in the history of the Washington Square Players. (Alexander Woollcott in *New York Times*, 19 Nov. 1916, Sec. II, p. 6)

It was the artistic success of this play which led to the formation of the Theatre Guild, a year and a half later, by members of the Players.[6] *Bushido*'s fame reached Japan. Michio Ito's old friend of European days, Kaoru Osanai, wrote from Tokyo asking for notes on the production and in particular on the way the role of Pine Tree was handled. Ito sent him all his notes and sketches, and Osanai performed Pine Tree in the New York way at the Shōgekijo theater in Tokyo.[7]

Less than a month after *Bushido*'s premiere, Michio Ito gave his first dance recital in the United States (6 December 1916). And now we step back into the dark ages. The USA was indeed a murky, barren land for artists, and not the least for dancers in those good old days when a big leap or an interminable pirouette was looked upon as the ultimate in terpsichore.[8] In his first recital Ito offered interpretations of both Japanese and European music.[9] The *New York Times* mentioned the costumes and set and listed titles of some of the dances, with no comment.[10] The writer on the *Tribune* singled out for his profound reflections one of Ito's most strikingly original compositions (to the *Pizzicati* of the *Sylvia* ballet music). He noted that "Mr. Itow pleased the audience mightily" with "a fantastic dance" in which "his gyrations were generally out of keeping with the spirit of the music, but they possessed a certain exotic appeal."[11] In ensuing years the Manhattan murk was to be dispelled, to some extent at least, by the persistent effort of one dancer—unsponsored, with no agent or promoter—just one serious artist working at his art.

The dancer who interprets music already familiar to an audience is likely to run up against a wall of prejudice, at least at first. Ito's ball dance, for example, alive with the exhilaration of chance's hazards, often

57

Pizzicatte   Michio.

SYMPHONIC DANCE POEMS

1931

MICHIO ITO

HAZEL WRIGHT ITO • JERRE
WALDEEN FALKENSTEIN • CHARLES TESKE

SOUVENIR PROGRAM

ABOVE:
Program cover with insignia inspired by Pizzicati
designed by J. T. Caldwell Tokyo 1931

confused and displeased the spectator for whom Chopin was bathed in moonlight, tubercle bacilli, and George Sand.[12]

Unperturbed by this kind of criticism, Ito gave another recital three months later (8 March 1917). Already a small dent was beginning to appear in the reportorial cranium on the *Times*. The *Tribune*'s intellect was still flailing in the darkness.

In early summer, 1917, Ito joined Adolph Bolm in a company known as Ballet Intime for a tour of East Coast cities on behalf of war charities.[13] Again, as in London, the beneficent influence of Ito's genius was felt by other artists, who in turn served as yeasty ferment to his own inspiration.

The young American pianist Charles T. Griffes, who had composed a musical setting for a dance drama staged by Irene Lewisohn,[14] was asked to write music for Ito's *Shō-Jō* or "The Spirit of Wine—A Symbol of Happiness," a dance previously performed by Ito to an old Japanese melody.[15] As Edward Maisel, Griffes' biographer, says, "The composer and his interpreter became good friends."[16] Griffes' letters echo his admiration and enthusiasm.[17] He applauded Ito's idea that Japanese music should be "brought into modified contact with Western influences"; and (in Maisel's words) "offered his own score (*Sho-Jo*) as a practical example of what this modified contact might mean."[18] Maisel further states that "Griffes composed for it [*Sho-Jo*] some of the most unusual music that he was ever to write."[19]

For some time Griffes had been trying, with little success, to get a hearing for his compositions.[20] *Sho-Jo* was, so to speak, a breakthrough. Musical critics would probably disclaim, but the fact seems to be that the dance interpretation made Griffes' music not only palatable but even comprehensible to the critics, as the following excerpts from reviews cited by Edward Maisel reveal:

Perhaps the most remarkable of the divertissements was Michio Ito's mime play, *Sho-Jo,* with music by . . . Charles Griffes.

A feature of the entertainment was *Sho-Jo,* a Japanese mime play, in which Michio Ito and Tulle Lindahl appeared. The music, composed by Charles T. Griffes, . . . proved especially interesting.

Ito in his Japanese intoxication that came out of no Broadway bottle.

Sho-Jo, a mime play, music by Charles Griffes, was one of the most gripping pieces of the evening.

From the musical standpoint the detail which stood forth in bold relief was the orchestration supplied by Charles T. Griffes for a pantomime done by Ito and Miss Lindahl.[21]

Maisel concludes: "Although Griffes did not succeed in getting Schirmer's to publish *Sho-Jo*, the whole episode had been a feather in his cap."

After a tour of other cities, Ballet Intime ended with a two weeks engagement at the Booth Theater in New York City. Griffes was a member of the company as composer, arranger, and accompanist; and from his letters, it appears, he thoroughly enjoyed the tour.[22]

In February 1918 Ito gave three recitals at which he danced to Griffes' arrangement of the Japanese melody *Sakura-Sakura*.[23] On February 26, the New York McDowell Club presented an evening of Charles Griffes' compositions, with Griffes at the piano. Among the selections was *Sho-Jo*, danced by Michio Ito, and five settings of Chinese lyrics to which Ito also danced.[24]

In April 1918 Ito gave three recitals as part of which he interpreted Griffes' *White Peacock*, with Charles Griffes at the piano.[25] Griffes had been trying for two years to obtain a favorable hearing and a critical review of this beautiful piece. As with *Sho-Jo*, it is apparent, Ito's dance created an audience for the music.[26] It was now on its way not only to critical acclaim but also to popularity. The following year (June 1919) it became a "featured number" at the Rivoli, danced by a protégée of Bolm's and Ito's to full orchestra conducted by Erno Rapé, with orchestral arrangement by the composer.[27]

Another talented young composer, an old friend of European days, Kōsaku Yamada, took part in the 1918 recitals. For the April program Ito created dances interpreting seven of Yamada's as yet unpublished com-

64

positions, three of them based on Noh music. Like Griffes, Yamada played his own compositions to accompany the dancers.[28]

Noh continued to hold its fascination for Michio Ito. Some of his dances were actually based on Noh themes: the mysterious fox spirit, the joyous spirit of wine in Shō-jō, the passion of jealous love in Dō-Jō-Ji. In March 1918 Ito appeared with Irene Lewisohn in Tamura, one of the Fenollosa-Pound translations.[29] Ito's staging was not strictly traditional. The chorus of twelve men sat on the side as in Noh, but they were masked and wore dark-blue kimonos and the high curved hat known as tate eboshi. And they spoke and chanted the actors' lines as well as their own.[30] Charles Griffes, who attended a performance, described his impression in a letter: "All the characters had on Japanese masks, and the whole thing gave a most strange and at the same time wonderful effect."[31]

On 10 July 1918 Ito presented William Butler Yeats's "Noh" play At the Hawk's Well, a production that, as already noted, aroused Yeats's curiosity. Dulac's masks, costumes, cloth, and screen were used as in the original London performance. But not the Dulac music: a new musical setting was composed by Kōsaku Yamada. Ito again played "the hawk"; the two other principal roles were taken by Japanese actors. Preceding the play there was a short program of Japanese music conducted by Yamada. The proceeds of the evening were donated to the Free Milk for France fund. The attendance was largely made up of dramatic critics and men and women of fashion who, it is reported, "laughed loudly and continuously" during the playing of the Japanese musical prelude, although the play was apparently well received.[32] The following month (August 1918) Ito and his Japanese performers toured the East Coast with a dance program that included At the Hawk's Well. Charles Griffes, who was of the company, not only played the accompaniment to dances, including his own Sho-Jo, but also helped Yamada with the playing of his Hawk's Well music.[33]

Although Ito did not at this time venture further into Noh drama, his dances, composed then and later, betray the influence that Noh continued to exert on his art. In August 1917 he had described his way of composing dances. It was his desire, he said, to bring together East and West in a style of his own. Like a sculptor he worked over every gesture until it meant what he would have it mean. "If you cry 'Stop!'" he explained, "in any place in my dance, you will find that it is a pose that

TULLE LINDAHL ~ TOSHI KOMORI
MICHIO ITOW
IN A SECOND SERIES OF RECITALS
AT THE
GREENWICH VILLAGE THEATRE
7th AVE & 4th STREET — SUNDAY NIGHTS — APRIL 7-14-21
TICKETS NOW ON SALE — TELEPHONE SPRING 6409
ENTIRE NEW PROGRAM

ABOVE:
Poster for recital   April   1918
Greenwich Village Theatre

RIGHT:
Ito modeling tate eboshi worn by Tamura chorus

66

Ito
as Boy in Tamura
Pound-Fenollosa
translation
Neighborhood Playhouse
New York
1918

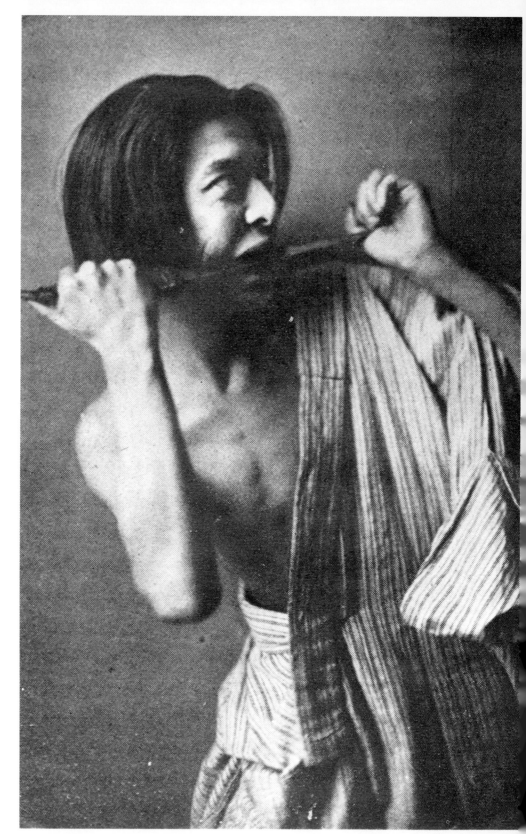

Michio Ito
soon after arrival
in New York
1916

68

means something. My *Spirit of Wine* dance is a joyous dance. . . . And my fox dance is furtive and independent and cunning and staccato. I studied a fox and his ways with a biscuit long before I worked out my dance. Then I went to a great hill in Hampstead and I made my soul into the soul of a fox, and so I evolved my fox dance."[34] We find in these words of his the same concern with "idea," with its expression in a definite, harmonious form, and the importance of meditation in bringing to perfection this marriage of form and idea in continuous movement.

Ito's dances are concrete illustrations of the Noh's essence as explained by Fenollosa:

> The beauty and power of Noh lie in the concentration. All elements—costume, motion, verse, and music—unite to produce a single clarified impression. Each drama embodies some primary human relation or emotion; and the poetic sweetness or poignancy of this is carried to its highest degree by carefully excluding all such obtrusive elements as a mimetic realism or vulgar sensationalism might demand. The emotion is always fixed upon idea, not upon personality.[35]

In performance Ito kept his face immobile so that personality was further excluded and idea enhanced. Though immobile, the face was not without expression; in harmony with the body it reflected the dance's idea. As Elizabeth Selden wrote of the impression made on her when she first saw Ito dance, "You can look at the dancer and no longer know whether it is man, woman, child, or angel dancing there."[36] In spite of the strong Noh influence, Ito's dance was, as he said, "his own." It was not Noh, not Japanese, but a distinctive creation combining East and West.

Within two years, fall 1916 to fall 1918, Michio Ito had presented in recital thirty different dances (solos, duets, small group dances) that I can definitely account for.[37] There were probably many more, perhaps twice that number. In addition the plays *Bushido, Hawk's Well,* and *Tamura* were presented.

From fall 1918 to June 1921 Ito apparently presented no dance concerts. He had begun to turn his talents in a new direction, again with novel and original effect. During the years 1919 to 1929 there appeared on the New York stage a series of revues, plays, musicals, and operettas, and an opera, all bearing the unmistakable Ito touch. These productions, 69 no matter how unsatisfactory in other respects, were praised for their visual beauty, particularly for telling rhythmic movement against settings perfect in simplicity and restraint. To quote from this criticism:

Greenwich Village Follies of 1919[38]

The color combinations, the light effects, the costumes, the grouping and posing, and the whole conception and spirit of the Ensembles are the best I have seen in a production of that nature. Indeed there are not many stage productions that I recall which match yours in sureness and individuality of artistic touch—which is all the more noteworthy because of the fine simplicity and economy of means employed to achieve the effects aimed at.[39]

What's in a Name[40]

Original and beautiful . . . every grouping takes on the appearance of a fine painting. . . .

There is a Watteau musical clock effect which is more beautiful than any musical comedy scene within memory, except the Japanese scene in the same piece, so ably staged by Michio Itow.[41]

Michio Itow's Pinwheel Revel[42]

Bright with a manner of dancing not seen elsewhere . . . new and artistic.[43]

For everyone except the confirmed seeker after the common-place.[44]

Its beauty and the simplicity of the show's settings. . . .[45]

Much is achieved visually with not much more scenery than could be carried on a bicycle.[46]

The little art gems of the talented Japanese, Michio Itow, thrive by their association only with their own kind.[47]

The Faithful[48]

Pictorially the play is always a delight . . . gorgeous setting . . . beautiful restraint in the settings . . . oriental quality in the settings.[49]

Arabesque[50]

[The movement in the village scene] became an integral . . . part of the whole action.

The scene of the wedding festivities . . . was not merely a carnival of rich color and movement. There was a logical unfolding of spectacular effect . . . also . . . a climactic progression in exotic visual thrills. Not the slightest of these were the . . . dances by a troupe of Arabians.[51]

Ito
in Greenwich Village Follies
1919

*Gypsy dance
in Greenwich Village
Follies
Ito and Serova*

72

LEFT:

*"In Old Japan"
sequence staged by
Michio Ito
for* What's in a Name
1920

BELOW:

*Set design
by Lee Simonson
for* The Faithful
1919

Bronze mask of Michio Ito by Isamu Noguchi   1926

[Fine effects] of moving figures. . . . The lanterns of the citizens go swirling and rushing over the town, everywhere, around, high, low, and their breathless lights upon the walls . . . infinitely extend the dramatic truth. The living figures now at the front, now at the back, now lighted, now silhouetted against light or dark, now singly, now in crowds; the shadows in their reds, purples, grays, yellows, blues; the management of the groups and movements; all these amplify our art of the theatre and carry it forward a long way. . . . Good or bad what we see in *Arabesque* is the work of genius. . . . And it is a virile art that we see.[52]

Sister Beatrice[53]
Michio Ito's study in black, white and gray for the rhythmic dance prolog . . . is instantly expressive of the religious atmosphere which is the keynote of the play.[54]

Goat Song[55]
. . . The mob scenes, however, merit the warmest commendation, for the Guild has not always excelled in ensemble direction. . . . the "charcoal burners, smugglers, Jews, Jewesses, landless men and women, gypsies, musicians and children" hang over the play as a diabolical threat and break loose as furies . . . against at least two striking settings by Lee Simonson.[56]

Turandot[57]
Colorful, exotic, picturesque; settings fearlessly fantastic without being elaborate . . . spirited, swiftly moving and of powerful effect.[58]

Cherry Blossoms[59]
Japanese operetta in the Shubert grand manner. Dances arranged in a truly Oriental style by Michio Ito.[60]

The settings are lavish and effective, that of the willow garden . . . really beautiful.[61]

Mikado[62]
Beautiful staging . . . charming chorus movements . . . magic promenades with lighted lanterns.[63]

Ames has surpassed all his other Gilbert and Sullivan revivals. . . . Against softly lit Hiroshige backgrounds the characters posture and dance in an exquisite blending of color values. If this revival were merely pantomime it would be worth traveling miles to see.[64]

. . . Almost positively the full stretch of winter ahead will not disclose another production of such mingled beauty and gaiety. . . .

The choruses he has turned over to Michio Ito, and they flow easily from one enchanting composition into another without ever having a self-conscious or stiff pictorial quality. They too have wit, and more than that they serve a constantly sensible and pliant purpose. They not only break out into diverting individual versions of the horn pipe to accompany Nanki-Poo's "A Wandering Minstrel I," but throughout the entire production they part and reunite in bewilderingly subtle patterns that give a fresh focus to their many scenes.[65]

Madame Butterfly[66]
The chorus achieved an excellent degree of movement and individuality.[67]

Settings and "business" have been worked out by Michio Ito.[68]

The Story of the Soldier (L'Histoire du Soldat)[69]
Quite the most pointedly effectual and brilliantly successful thing the League of Composers has done. . . . There is indeed little use trying to label it, for it is uniquely in a class by itself. If anything, it is pantomime with a chamber orchestra accompaniment and the part of a narrator of the proceedings thrown in. . . .

It was supposed, when Stravinsky's music for this tale was given here four years ago by the League without the accompanying stage action, that the pantomime was incidental to the score, that the score itself was the main consideration. But last Sunday it appeared very plainly that the boot was on the other foot. None the less, the music which four years ago seemed astonishingly unimportant and ineffective, now gained the force of its background, the color of its real purpose. . . .

Michio Ito, the Japanese, who was responsible for some of the best direction the American Opera Company displayed while it was here, had the chief hand in the production of "The Story of the Soldier." He managed something that was homogeneous and striking, something that came across the footlights with definition. And it embodied peculiarly what Stravinsky and Ramuz had in their heads. . . .[70]

We know that Ito had a hand in all the above productions. The extent of his participation, however, is not always clear, because others sometimes accepted, with great complacence, praise called forth by his work.

But, from the remarkable similarity in the critics' reactions to these various pieces of theater, one is tempted to conclude that Ito's role in each instance was a large one. However that may be, Michio Ito was not one to worry about kudos. Realization of his ideas counted for more with him. And, as it turned out, the experience of directing the movement of large groups in those plays, musicals, and operas was to stand him in good stead when he moved on to his great symphonic interpretations in California.

Ito did not abandon his own style of dance during those years (1919-1929). In 1927 and 1928, even as he busied himself with the theatrical ventures described above, his inventive genius burst forth in a profusion of his own lyrical dance poems. During those two years alone he presented more than forty new dances in recital. Recitals in 1920 and 1923 had already increased his repertory by nine dances, and his *Pinwheel Revel* (1922) added a few more. Ted Shawn wrote that in those years "Michio Ito [was] constantly presenting premieres of new works. Ito, a Japanese, was truly one of the American modern dance pioneers: at one time he took a Broadway theater and presented full evenings of dance with many guest artists from the contemporary American dance field, and provided the friendly environment to develop much new and valuable talent—Angna Enters made some of her first appearances in Michio Ito's *Pinwheel*."[71]

Along with other productions, Ito acted in a repetition of the Noh play *Tamura* (1921) and in *She Who Was Fished* and *The Fox's Grave*, kyōgen translated by him in collaboration with Louis V. Ledoux (1923),[72] and appeared as a guest artist with other dancers.[73] It might seem that Michio Ito would have no time for other pursuits, but he did. Dissatisfaction both with the economic situation of dancers and with the lack of theaters in which to rehearse and perform drove him to agitate for a dancers' guild and for a foundation that was to build and maintain an edifice with theaters in which there might be a fusion of theatrical arts: drama, poetry, music, dance, and so on. He was, apparently, making headway with this plan when, like so many other artistic projects, it was swept under by the 1929 crash.[74]

Above all else, Ito was a teacher. During his years in New York he taught, in his own studio and in those of others, and presented his pupils in their own and in his recitals. Some critics, like Nickolas Muray, deprecated Ito's use of students: "None [of the assisting artists] had arrived at the peak of Ito's perfection, as the contrast obviously proved. It must be that Ito had a definite reason of his own for this retiring attitude and giving a chance to his pupils to assert publicly their talent. Which of course is most generous of him, but should not have been at the expense of the interested public."[75] A number of these pupils, however—Lester Horton, Nimura, Pauline Koner, Angna Enters—came to occupy a respectable place in the dance world as competent professionals.[76]

Early in 1929 Michio Ito left New York with a small group of pupils to appear in recital in cities throughout the United States.[77] The tour ended in Los Angeles, with a dance concert on 28 April 1929 at the Figueroa Playhouse. Michio Ito did not return to New York but remained in California for the next thirteen years.

IV California and the Symphonies

That first concert was, at least for some of us, the bright omen long awaited but little hoped for. Today, after all these years, many of the dancers' gestures, much of their movement, and even whole dances remain, as it were, in a special compartment of my brain where I can look at them at will, as if they were actually before me in all their fresh beauty of line and color, from Dorothy Wagner's tall blonde grace in *Ecclesiastique* to Michio Ito's final jet-black *Pizzicati* with its mystifying power.[1]

The audience that night comprised mostly artists, among them dancers. And within a matter of days Michio Ito was teaching two classes in a Hollywood studio:[2] a master class attended by professional dancers and a second class which he called "community dance." That is a class for anyone. Ito believed that everyone could and should dance, that dancing was good for both body and mind and created a balance between them, and that it was, as Laurence Binyon said of art, "a means to beauty in life."[3]

Accordingly, Ito's community class was made up of writers, musicians, sculptors, teachers, and simple amateurs of various arts, persons who had no intention or desire to become professional dancers but who wanted to acquire aesthetic balance and to better understand, through the art of dance, all art. Ito scorned making art incomprehensible, remote, a secret thing for the few, and he accused those who would of hiding ignorance   79

At the Hawk's Well
Argus Bowl   1929   Harpist and chorus

OPPOSITE PAGE   *top to bottom:*
Katherine Stubergh, Beatrix Baird,
Mary Jane Mayhew, Helen Caldwell
Photograph by Toyo Miyatake

BELOW   *left to right:*
Mary Jane Mayhew, Beatrix Baird, Helen Caldwell,
Katherine Stubergh.
This photograph by Toyo Miyatake
was hung in the London Salon of Photography
of 1930

PAGES 82-83:
Argus Bowl Rehearsal group   1929
Top row left to right:
Helen Caldwell, Paul Nidate, Katherine Stubergh.
Second row:
Dorothy Wagner, Dolores Lopez, Beatrix Baird, Michio Ito.
Foreground: Toyo Miyatake

81

behind subterfuge. "Everyone can be an artist in movement," he de-
clared. "Balance is attainable by all."[4] Indeed, I think I never saw him
more joyously excited than on the occasion when, after some of us had
given a brief program for a multitudinous square-dance society in Long
Beach Municipal Auditorium, he looked out from the stage on hundreds
of old men and women below dancing to piano and corn fiddle.

Ito loved to teach, because of these beliefs and for another reason.
There was nothing of the exhibitionist about him; he would rather see his
dances performed by others than do them himself. The dances as creations were more important to him than his own dancing. When one is
performing a dance he cannot see that dance; and dance is primarily a
visual art. It is to be noted that even before he came to California he had
ceased to compose dances for himself.[5]

Members of his master class soon appeared with him in a series of
Monday evening recitals (5 August to 2 September 1929) in Argus Bowl,
Eagle Rock. Besides his own dance poems, he presented two *kyōgen*
which he had translated in collaboration with Louis V. Ledoux[6] and the
William Butler Yeats, "Noh" play, *At the Hawk's Well.*

Although *At the Hawk's Well* was mounted with a far greater sophisti-
cation than that of the chandelier-lit drawing room advocated by Yeats, it
still had no theatricality in the usual sense; the effect was poetic simplicity. Argus Bowl was a small Greek-style theater in a hillside on the Argus
estate. It seated about three hundred persons. High above the actors one
saw in dim outline the jagged peaks of a sierra. All around in the dark
were trees. And there was a wizard named Lewis Barrington behind the
lights to give the scene that otherworld reality Yeats had sought.[7] This
new setting still called upon the spectator's imagination, with its black

85

night, the faint suggestion of hills, and light that seemed a part of the verse. The hawk-guardian of the well was played by Lester Horton, a young dancer in Ito's master class. He also made the costumes for the three principals. The music used was Dulac's; besides the chorus, there was a harp and an oboe, and Ito played the drums and cymbals.[8] The performance was open to the general public but actually the attendance consisted mainly of artists and amateurs of the arts. Yeats would have been pleased.

At the very time Ito was presenting these small, finely wrought gems in Argus Bowl to an elite audience of artists and intellectuals, he was preparing a grand essay at interpretation of symphonic music. On 20 September 1929, little more than two weeks after the final evening in Argus Bowl, he presented two hundred dancers with symphonic orchestra and choruses in the Pasadena Rose Bowl.[9] The music interpreted by his choreographies was Tchaikovsky's *Andante Cantabile*, two Chopin waltzes, Grieg's *Peer Gynt Suite*, and Dvorak's *New World Symphony*. The dances, as well as the music they represented visually, were symphonic in nature with different groups of dancers carrying the different musical themes.

In May 1928 Ito had taken part, along with Benjamin Zemach and Martha Graham, in a performance of a somewhat similar nature, to music by Debussy. It was one of three "orchestral dramas" presented by Alice and Irene Lewisohn at the Manhattan Opera House, with the Cleveland Symphony Orchestra under the baton of Nikolai Sokoloff.[10] Both the Rose Bowl presentation and the orchestral dramas found their source in Jaques-Dalcroze's dance-music idea as realized by him in his 1912, 1913, and 1914 productions.[11] But Ito's work at Pasadena, while true to Dalcroze's ideal, surpassed both the Dalcroze and the Lewisohn performances, for in his choreographies there was no pantomime or realistic representation of any sort to distract the mind from the music's charm; as always with Ito, music and dance were at one.[12]

Most of the dances were performed by women. Their costumes of flowing white silk with bodices in varied pastel shades of velveteen could be used without change for the several pieces of music. The men wore shaggy brown caveman-style tunics and shaggy wigs in the *Hall of the Mountain King* and, for the *New World Symphony*, costumes suggestive of woodsmen and of Indians. There was one solo by Ito himself, his

Dorothy Wagner in Andante Cantabile   Pasadena Rose Bowl   1929
Photographs by Toyo Miyatake

Pizzicati to the *Sylvia* ballet music. A gold folding screen forty feet high and one hundred twenty-five feet long served as backdrop for all the dancing.

The occasion was the Pageant of Lights to mark the installation in the stadium of the largest sun arcs ever used,[13] but the purpose was artistic. In the words of the sponsoring organization, "It was felt that in keeping with the artistic idea of the lights a program should be presented in keeping with the most artistic aspirations of the city. It is the most costly entertainment ever given in the Rose Bowl and will in a large measure determine whether elaborate pageants of this type are to be continued or not, depending on the success of the feature."[14]

The result exceeded expectations. These sentences extracted from a long, ecstatic review give a hint of the impression created:

Big Pageant is Marked Success

A slim black figure, silhouetted in startling relief against an enormous gold screen, dominated the Rose Bowl and held a crowd of five thousand people spellbound and silent, as Michio Ito, Japanese dancer, performed his famous shadow dance. . . .

From the moment the huge new floodlights were turned on . . . a uniquely beautiful and stirring pageant held the spectators' attention.

The forty-foot gold screen, which served as background, was so illuminated by searchlights that startling color effects and combinations were constantly thrown upon it, and as the white-robed dancers advanced from behind this screen over the green field, the effect was of some scene from ancient Greek mythology. . . .

Michio Ito's Shadow Dance was the climax of the program. Poised above and behind the orchestra, the searchlights . . . threw the shadow of his body upon the screen behind him. The hushed admiration of the crowd and the soft strains of "Pizzicati" from the

musicians, all centered about the graceful figure. His dominance of the Bowl was the dominance of the artist. The dance in itself was extraordinary, with only the upper portion of the body, the arms and head serving as a medium of expression. Recalled to the stage he performed the dance a second time, and the audience gave every indication of being willing to see it as many times as he could be induced to perform it. . . .

As the first time in the West that a night program with appropriate lighting has been attempted, the Pageant of Lights could only be described as more than fulfilling the expectations of those who have worked so many months to make the project a successful one.[15]

Pasadena's artistic purpose—that the Pageant of Lights be the first in a never-ending series—was doomed to disappointment. The city fathers had not reckoned with the economic crash and failing banks which came little more than a month later. Their grandiose idea, like Ito's plan for a theatric arts foundation, vanished under its impact. There was never again a "pageant of lights" in the Rose Bowl.

In spite of the depression, however, and a tiny budget, Ito presented in Hollywood Bowl on 15 August 1930 a symphonic choreography that was a distinct artistic advance over the more hastily prepared Rose Bowl pageant of the year before. He used one hundred twenty-five dancers in an interpretation of the Polovetski dances from Borodin's *Prince Igor.*

Hollywood Bowl's geography had always been a kind of death trap for choreographers. The huge auditorium even then seated twenty thousand persons, so that beyond its first small section unclad arms and legs resembled nothing so much as little sausages. Add to this the strange terrain on which the dancers had to perform. Ito overcame both obstacles and turned them to his advantage. His dancers' costumes were calculated by cut and color to conquer distance and enhance gestures and group movements. They were of cheap cotton cloth but in bold patterns of brilliant color: trousers, full, sleeved tunics, sashes, headdresses—the women's with long veils—boots of bright-colored oilcloth. Michio's brother Kisaku Ito[16] had come from Japan to design and superintend the making of costumes that carried the powerful beauty of his brother's art to the farthest reaches of that vast auditorium.

In those days the dancing place was made up of several parts: first a straight, narrow space adjoining the orchestra's stage; then, also running

91

At rehearsal
for Prince Igor
1930
From left:
Ralph Faulkner,
one of the dancers,
Michio Ito,
Edith Jane

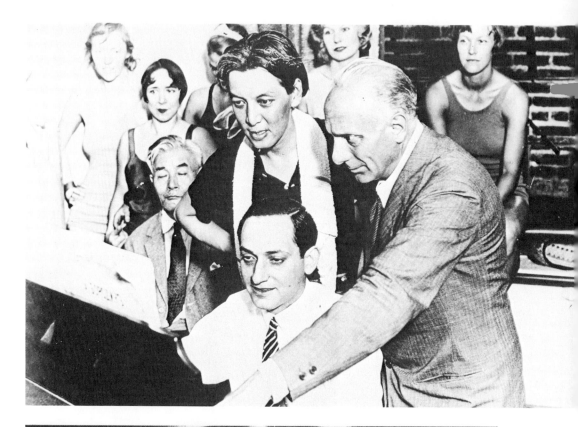

ABOVE:
Rehearsal
for Prince Igor
1930
Michio Ito,
Bernardino
Molinari,
Raymond Sachse
at the piano

RIGHT:
1930
Hollywood
Bowl Season

NINTH ANNUAL PROGRAM
GUEST CONDUCTORS

Alfred Hertz....July 8-10-11-12   Bernardino Molinari,.........   Pietro Cimini...........Aug. 19
Karl Krueger, July 15-17-18-19   July 22 to Aug. 15   Enrique Arbos....Aug. 21 to 30

GUEST SOLOISTS

Margaret Matzenauer....July 11   Michio Ito..........Aug. 15
Richard Crooks.........July 18   Albertina Rasch.........Aug. 1   Kathleen Parlow.......Aug. 22
Elsa Alsen............July 25   Percy Grainger.........Aug. 8   Alfred Wallenstein.....Aug. 29

the width of the stage, a flight of eight steps led to a flat, narrow, curved space planted in grass and enclosed by a four-foot hedge; six more steps led to another curved green, which was separated from the audience by a low wall or curb. The whole space from orchestra to audience was extremely narrow for a large number of performers.

In Ito's dance symphony, these levels gradually filled with the different groups, differently costumed, which interpreted the various musical themes or ideas. (Even the bothersome hedge four feet high and two feet across became a part of the Polovetski camp as barbaric men leapt across it with enormous spears.) The strong, definite gestures and the long movements of the groups were clearly visible on the different stage levels. The musical themes they interpreted united in a complex whole, yet remained distinct as in the music itself. Dance and music were one.

As usual with Ito, he had aroused musicianly admiration and sympathy. The orchestra conductor, Bernardino Molinari, attended most of the rehearsals from the very beginning, enthusiastically conferring with Ito and often playing piano accompaniment for the dancers.[17] The happy result may be gleaned in the following excerpts from reviews:

> At least 20,000 persons wedged their way into Hollywood Bowl last night to see Michio Ito's ballet and to hear Bernardino Molinari direct the orchestra. . . .
> Ito's choreographic art made them glad they came. He visualized the dances from Borodin's "Prince Igor" in a barbaric pageant of motion and color. Gauze drapes with stylized design were drawn in front of the orchestra shell. This . . . device eliminated the players from the picture without making them grope for their notes by the inadequate lighting of desk lamps, as it has sometimes been their misfortune to do. The corps de ballet . . . was divided into groups, each one . . . following the various inner voices of the music.
> The Japanese director contrived a genuine symphony of movement, unconventional in its vocabulary of gesture and of absorbing, exciting interest. The whole spectacle was a triumph of gorgeousness that inspires the hope for others of the kind. Such an artist as Ito is an asset to the community.[18]

> Michio Ito and his ballet were given a veritable ovation by a crowd that overflowed the Bowl and filled every available standing space on the hillsides last night. The ensemble was particularly fine, and parti-colored costumes that enabled instantaneous change of color

patterns according to the angle presented by the dancers were exceptionally effective.

. . . Clever use was made of the shape of the setting, for which the dance was obviously created, and the scene was a riot of ever changing colors, patterns and rhythms. [These] figures revolved with continuous symmetry.[19]

There have been many ballets at the Bowl, but never such a beautiful one as that presented and staged by the Japanese artist.

Instead of running foot races, or forming pretty pictures, Ito and his dancers threw themselves headlong into a strict interpretation of Borodin's ballet music from "Prince Igor." . . .

The dancers clad in gorgeous oriental dress—costumes that were partly Russian, Chinese, Persian, and Arabian—presented a fascinating ensemble against the gauze drapes drawn in front of the orchestra shell.

These drapes, black at the far end, white and painted with a striking tree design in the center, served both as background and a means to shut off sight of the black-coated orchestra which would have been wholly out of keeping with the dance and the colorful dress of the dancers.

Ito . . . is a splendid asset to the community. May he and his dancers be called upon often to perform at the Bowl.[20]

Ito's next venture into this type of choreography was Gluck's opera *Orpheus*, presented in Redlands Bowl on 26 June 1936. Again a scrim was drawn before the orchestra, chorus, and principal singers, while the dancers interpreted the music and its themes with formal gesture. The number of dancers was smaller, only thirty-five; the choreography, like the music, was simple in design but exquisite.[21]

Ito's final opportunity to realize interpretation of symphonic music came in 1937, again in Hollywood Bowl, again with the Los Angeles Philharmonic Orchestra. And again he used the Bowl's peculiar drawbacks to enhance his work. On 19 August he presented two dance interpretations to music widely different in nature: the eighth-century Japanese *Etenraku (Music Coming Through Heaven)* and Strauss's *Blue Danube Waltz*.

The orchestra was conducted by Hidemaro Konoye, who, at Ito's urging, had composed an orchestration for *Etenraku*; it is now regarded as Konoye's finest work.[22] Performed against a long gold folding screen,

LEFT:

Hazel Wright Ito
in Little Shepherdess
1931

BELOW:

Hazel Wright Ito
Photographs by Toyo Miyatake

Etenraku was heavily and gorgeously costumed in a style faintly reminiscent of ancient Japan, but with colors suggesting sunset, clouds, wind and snow, mountain foliage, and sea. The dance itself was no more Japanese than Ito's "Japanese" solos described above, indeed, not so much so, for the music is more abstract and so too were the gestures of the dance. A more beautiful, more perfect marriage of music and dance is hard to conceive of, but at that time Japanese music was little appreciated in this country. Besides, the shadow of Manchuria had already fallen over most things Japanese.

Ito's *Blue Danube* was a tour de force. It had in its composition many forms of ballroom dance from many periods, not only waltzes but also minuets, mazurkas, polkas, gavottes, what not, incorporated into long lines of spirited movement to revive in the spectator the joy of a dearly remembered ball, or of all the balls and parties one had ever heard or read about. The *Blue Danube* was repeated in Hollywood Bowl that September with a smaller orchestra (fifty musicians), and Ito added two new symphonic choreographies interpreting two unpublished Mozart minuets.[23]

For Ito, dance was inseparable from music. Although he might avail himself of the artistic principles and technique of Japanese Noh and Kabuki, he considered his own dance Western because of its marriage with music. "When I dance," he said, "the music does not accompany me—we become as one. Sometimes the instrument has the melody, sometimes I have it, and sometimes the melodies are intertwined."[24]

The background of Japanese dancing, in Ito's words, is literature; that of Western dancing is music. In both instances dance is used as a medium of expressing human thought and emotion. But Western dancing produces a more abstract effect, for in the accompanying music the spectator is left free to imagine what the dance is saying, while in dance accompanied by poetry (or prose) the effect is concrete and definite since the description is given in words.[25] During his recitals Ito had noted that his dances created different impressions on different members of the audience. This, he decided, was because of the individual's turn of mind and experience, so that both dance movement and music called up different thoughts and emotions from the memories and imaginations of the various spectators.[26]

The highest form of this abstract art was, in Ito's own opinion, attained by him in the choreographic symphonies performed in California. And

LEFT: Michio Ito   1929

DIRECTLY BELOW:
Michio and Hazel Ito
in his Hollywood Studio   1931

BELOW:
Arrival of Ito's company in Tokyo April 1931.
At his left his wife, their children, Donald and Gerald,
at the side and in front of Ito

OPPOSITE PAGE   *ABOVE:*

Ecclesiastique IV   Rehearsal at Pasadena Playhouse   1931
Photograph by Toyo Miyatake

OPPOSITE PAGE   *BELOW:*

Etenraku rehearsal in Hollywood Bowl   1937
Gold folding screen in background   Photograph by Toyo Miyatake

BELOW: Etenraku costumes

RIGHT:
Michio Ito and his elder son,
Donald (aet. 13)
Snapshot by Barbara Perry   1937

OPPOSITE PAGE:
"To send home to my mother"
Michio Ito   1929
Photograph by Toyo Miyatake

BELOW:
Swimming party at Perry Studio   1937
Hidemaro Konoye in dark glasses;
Ito at his right;
Gerald Ito, Michio's younger son,
in extreme right lower corner

ABOVE:
Caricature of Konoye by Ito   1937

RIGHT:
Viscount Hidemaro Konoye
Photograph by Toyo Miyatake

he hailed the invention of the pentatonic and diatonic scales on which "powerful structures of music have been reared, and rendered by the modern large, but responsive, orchestra, inviting every fancy of the emotions." "But," he concluded, "progressive as we have been in developing dance and music, we have only entered the threshold of the art in its purest form."[27]

Since a dancer does not live by art alone but also "by bread and the appurtenances thereto," Michio Ito taught classes throughout the depression days of the thirties. He gave recitals at frequent intervals in cities throughout California and twice in Japan.[28] For these, he composed at least fifteen new dance poems and a "ballet pastorale" to music specially written for him by W. Franke Harling.[29] He composed and directed dance sequences for three motion pictures[30] and directed dances and movement of singers and choruses for an opera.[31] He adapted Japanese dramas for the American and European stage and directed their performance by Japanese companies.[32] All the above activities partook in varying degrees of Ito's distinctive art, but they were overshadowed by the powerful beauty of his symphonic choreographies.

A strange country and a Great Depression had not prevented Michio Ito from fulfilling at least a part of his destiny, which was, I believe, to foster or arouse the creative spirit in other artists—artists of all sorts, not only dancers—and even in those among the general public who did not yet know their own ability. Needless to mention the pleasure his dances gave to thousands, for, like all great art, his creations left the beholder with a feeling of exhilaration.

Ito's last appearance on the California scene was when he presented his sister-in-law Teiko Ito in a dance recital on 8 November 1941.[33]

Following Pearl Harbor all Japanese were evacuated from the West Coast. After a brief internment Michio Ito returned to Japan on the *Gripsholm*. His two children were removed to New York by their uncle Yuji Ito, who was a resident of that city.

After the war Michio Ito was active in the theater in Japan; but that was another career, another story. It would seem that his old, beautiful muse had vanished in the Japan of Tojo and Douglas MacArthur.

APPENDIXES

Appendix I

A. *For Solo Performance unless Otherwise Noted*

COMPOSER AND MUSIC	DANCE TITLE
Albéniz, Isaac	
Malagueña	*Malagueña* (1928)
Seguidilla	*Bullfighter* (1920)
Tango in D	**Tango* (1927)
Bach	
Gavotte in E	*Gavotte* (1923)
Beethoven	
Minuet	*Minuet* (1937)
?	*Harlequin and Columbine* (duet) (1935)
Sonata (?)	*Sonata* (1931)

Note: Since all the dances are interpretations of music, it was found convenient to list them by musical composers. Year of first performance in the United States is given in parentheses. Dances marked by an asterisk are described in chapter one. Some of these dances were later arranged, or composed anew, by Ito for group performance.

COMPOSER AND MUSIC	DANCE TITLE
Boccherini	
Menuet in A	*Minuet
Chopin	
Étude op. 10 no. 9	*Chopin Étude (1929)
(F minor)	
Nocturne op. 15 no. 2	*Ball (1928)
(F-sharp)	
Waltz op. 64 no.2	*Ladybug (1929)
(C-sharp minor)	
Waltz (E-flat)	Waltz (duet) (1928)
Waltz (?)	Mermaid (1929)
Couperin	
Sarabande	Sarabande (1927)
Debussy	
Deuxième Arabesque	*Arabesque II (3 dancers) (1928)
Clair de Lune	Clair de Lune (1933)
Children's Corner VI,	*Golliwogg's Cakewalk (1917)
Golliwogg's Cakewalk	
Children's Corner V,	*Little Shepherdess (1928)
Little Shepherd	
Petite Suite I, En Bateau	En Bateau (1929)
Petite Suite II, Cortège	Cortège (1931)
Petite Suite III, Menuet	Debussy Minuet (1936)
Prelude VIII, La Fille aux	*Maid with the Flaxen Hair
Cheveux de Lin	(1937)
?	Shadow (1929)
Delibes	
Passepied (Le Roi S'Amuse)	*Passepied (1927)
Pizzicati (Sylvia Ballet)	Pizzicati (1916)
Font y de Anta	
?	Portuguese Country Dance (1928)

COMPOSER AND MUSIC	DANCE TITLE

Griffes
  Sho-Jo (Spirit of Wine)
  The White Peacock op. 7 no. 1
	Sho-Jo (Spirit of Wine) (1917)
	*White Peacock (1918)

Harling Poem no. 1	Birth of the Soul (1931)

Ippolitov-Ivanov
  Caucasian Sketches no. 2,
    In the Village
	*Caucasian Dance (1929)

Kelley Lady Picking Mulberries	*Javanese Dance (1928)
Lully Sarabande	Sarabande (1929)
Middleton ?	Down South (1928)
Ornstein Wild Men's Dance	Wild Men's Dance (1918)

Puccini
  Madame Butterfly
	Japanese Girl on Cherry
	  Tree Hill (1916)

Rachmaninoff ?	Warrior (1928)
Rameau La Joyeuse	La Joyeuse (1927)

Ravel
  Ma Mère L'Oye III,
    Impératrice des Pagodes
	*Impression of a Chinese
	  Actor (1926)

Rimsky-Korsakov ?	Hymn to the Sun (1927)

Poster for 1931 recital   Design by Michio Ito

COMPOSER AND MUSIC	DANCE TITLE
Saint-Saëns	
?	*Spirit Escaping from Bondage* (1916)
Sarasate	
Op. 21 no. 2, Habanera	*Habanera* (1929)
Op. 21 no. 1, Malagueña	*Spanish Fan Dance* (1929)
Satie	
Gnossienne no. 1	*Gnossienne I* (1933)
Gnossienne no. 2	*Gnossienne II* (1934)
Sawada	
Genroku Hanamiodori	*Japanese Spring Dance* (1918)
Schumann	
Études Symphoniques, op.13, Theme	*Ecclesiastique I* (1922)
Études Symphoniques, op. 13, Var. I	*Warrior* (1928)
Études Symphoniques, op. 13, Var. II	*Tragedy* (1931)
Études Symphoniques, op. 13, Var. III	*Friendship* (5 dancers) (1931)
Études Symphoniques, op. 13, Var. IV	*Joy* (1928)
Scott, Cyril	
Indian Suite no. 4	*Dancing Girl* (1933)
Lotus Land op. 47, no. 1	*Lotus Land* (1928)
?	*Bird Dance* (1918)
?	*Mandarin Ducks* (duet) (1928)
?	*Song of India* (1920
Scriabin	
Caresse Dansée op. 57 no. 2	*Caresse*
Preludes, op. 11 no. 4	*Prelude IV* (1930)

Ito as Pierrot in his pantomime-play The Donkey *(?)*

COMPOSER AND MUSIC	DANCE TITLE
Preludes, op. 11 no. 5	*Prelude V (1927)
Preludes, op. 11 no. 6	*Prelude VI (1927)
Preludes, op. 11 no. 8	*Prelude VIII (1927)
Preludes, op. 11 no. 9	*Prelude IX (1927)
Preludes, op. 11 no. 10	*Prelude X (1927)
Preludes, op. 11 no. 11	Prelude XI (1930)
Preludes, op. 11 no. 15	Prelude XV (8 dancers) (1930)
Smetana	
Polkas	Polka (1928)
Stravinsky (see App. 2)	
Tchaikovsky	
?	A Fable—A Chinese Dance (1918)
Andante Cantabile op. 11	Ecclesiastique II (6 dancers) (1928) (see also App. 1, B)
	Ecclesiastique IV (13 dancers) (1931)
Nutcracker Suite	Danse de la Fée Dragée (1927)
	Danse Chinoise (1927)
	Danse Arabe (1927)
	Danse des Fleurs (1927)
	Marche des Mirlitons (1927)
Verdi (see App. 2)	
Yamada	
The Blue Flame (Oto no Nagare no. 6)	The Blue Flame (1918)
Crane and Tortoise	Tsuru Kame (2 dancers) (1918)
	*Pair of fans (1927)
Four Seasons in Kyoto	Kyō-no-Shiki (1918)
	*Single Fan (1927)
Fukagawa Bushi (popular dance)	Fukagawa Bushi (1918)

Ito in
The Blue Flame (?)

COMPOSER AND MUSIC	DANCE TITLE
Kappore (peasant dance)	*Kappore* (3 dancers) (1918)
Song of the Plovers	*Chidori no Kyoku* (1918)
O Edo (Travellers' Chorus) (Suite Japonaise no. 2)	*Spring Rain* (1928)
Oto no Nagare (Stream of Tone) no. 1	*Tone Poem I* (1928)
Oto no Nagare (Stream of Tone) no. 8	*Tone Poem II* (1928)
Oto no Nagare (Stream of Tone) no. 10	*Faun* (1928)
Yari no Odori (Dance with a Spear	*Yari no Odori* (1918)
NATIVE MUSIC	
Burmese melody arr. by Michio Ito	*Burmese Temple Dance* (3 dancers) (1928)
Pavane (16-cent. English)	*Pavane* (1928)
Hindu melody	*Sari Dance* (1928)
"Dō-Jō-Ji," Japanese melody arr. by Lassalle Spier	*Dō-Jō-Ji* (1918)
"Echigo-Jishi," Japanese melody arr. by Lassalle Spier	*Echigo-Jishi* (1918)
Japanese melody	*Female Demon* (1917)
Japanese melody	*Fox Dance* (1917)
Japanese melody	*Japanese Spear Dance* (1923)
"Kawanaka Jina Kogun Funto," Japanese chanted poem	*Kembu (Sword Dance)* (1918)
Japanese melody arr. by Lassalle Spier	*Matsu-no-Midori* (1918)
Japanese melody	*Odori* (1918)
"Sakura-Sakura," Japanese melody arr. by Charles T. Griffes	*Sakura-Sakura* (1917)

COMPOSER AND MUSIC	DANCE TITLE
"Shō-jō," Japanese melody (Griffes later composed music "Sho-Jo" for which Ito created a new dance; s.v. Griffes, above.)	Spirit of Wine (1916)
Persian melody arr. by Michio Ito	Persian Fantasy (1928)
Siamese melody	Siamese Dance (1921)
MUSIC NOT IDENTIFIED	Blue Boy (1927) Blue Waves (1923) Chinese Buffoon (1921) Chinese Spear (1927) Gypsy Dance (1921) Jazz and Jazz (small group) (1922) Lilies of the Field (6 dancers) (1922) Marionette (1916) Tropical Night (small group) (1922)

B. Symphonic Choreographies Performed to Full Orchestra

COMPOSER AND MUSIC	DANCE TITLE
Borodin Polovetski Dances, Prince Igor	Prince Igor (125 dancers) (1930) Hollywood Bowl
Chopin Waltz op. 18 (E-flat)	Waltz (50 dancers) (1929) Pasadena Rose Bowl

COMPOSER AND MUSIC	DANCE TITLE
Waltz op. 64 no. 2 (C-sharp minor)	*Waltz* (30 dancers) (1929) Pasadena Rose Bowl
Dvorak Symphony no. 5 *(From the New World)*	*New World Symphony* (100 dancers) (1929) Pasadena Rose Bowl
Gluck Orpheus	*Orpheus* (35 dancers) (1936) Redlands Bowl

Grieg
Peer Gynt Suite
	Peer Gynt Suite (90 dancers) (1929) Pasadena Rose Bowl
	  1. Morning (30 dancers)
	  2. Anitra's Dance (30 dancers)
	  3. Hall of the Mountain King (30 dancers)

Harling Mary Magdalene (ballet pastorale especially composed for Michio Ito)	*Mary Magdalene* (18 dancers) (1931) Los Angeles Philharmonic Auditorium
Ippolitov-Ivanov Caucasian Sketches, Cortège du Sardar	*Cortège du Sardar* (32 dancers) (1933) Greek Theater, Los Angeles
Mozart Two unpublished menuettos	*Two Minuets* (32 dancers) (1937) Hollywood Bowl

COMPOSER AND MUSIC	DANCE TITLE

Strauss
  The Blue Danube Waltz
	Blue Danube (48 dancers)
	  (1937) Hollywood Bowl

Tchaikovsky
  Andante Cantabile op. 11
	Ecclesiastique III (1929)
	  Pasadena Rose Bowl

Eighth- or ninth-century
Japanese (?) composer
  Etenraku (Music Coming
    Through Heaven), orchestrated
    by Hidemaro Konoye
	Etenraku (22 dancers) (1937)
	  Hollywood Bowl

Appendix 2

TITLE	PLACE AND DATE OF PRODUCTION
A. Plays	
Arabesque by C. Head and E. Tietjens	New York, 1925
At the Hawk's Well by William Butler Yeats	London, 1916; New York, 1918; Eagle Rock, 1929
Bushido by Takeda Izumo	New York, 1916
The Donkey by Michio Ito (see sec. C)	
The Faithful by John Masefield	New York, 1919
Goat Song by Franz Werfel	New York, 1926
Kabuki—Children's Theater	Los Angeles and New York, 1932
Kyōgen—The Fox's Grave (Kitsune Zuka)	Eagle Rock, 1929
Kyōgen—She Who Was Fished (Tsuri-Onna)	New York, 1923

TITLE	PLACE AND DATE OF PRODUCTION
Kyōgen—Somebody Nothing (*Busu*)	Eagle Rock, 1929
Samurai and Geisha (18th-cent. dramas)	Los Angeles and New York, 1930
Sister Beatrice by Maurice Maeterlinck	New York, 1926 (?)
Tamura	New York, 1918 and 1921
Turandot by Carl Gozzi	New York, 1929

B. Operas and Operettas

Madame Butterfly by Puccini	Washington, 1927 New York, 1928
Histoire du Soldat (see sec. D)	
La Traviata by Verdi	Los Angeles, 1936
Cherry Blossoms, book and lyrics by Harry B. Smith, score by Sigmund Romberg	New York, 1927
The Mikado by Gilbert and Sullivan	New York, 1927

C. Pantomimes

The Donkey by Michio Ito*	New York, 1918
Mary Magdalene, music by W. Franke Harling	Los Angeles, 1931

*This mime included in its cast a toy donkey. On 21 December 1935 Yeats wrote Lady Wellesley about a play he was working on (*The Herne's Egg*), in which one of the personages was a toy donkey (*Letters on Poetry from W. B. Yeats to Dorothy Wellesley* [London: Oxford University Press, 1964]). Were these donkeys related? Were they both born in 1915–16?

TITLE	PLACE AND DATE OF PRODUCTION
D. Pantomime-Play-Dance	
The Story of the Soldier (L'Histoire du Soldat), music by Igor Stravinsky, book by C. F. Ramuz	New York, 1928
E. Musical Revues	
Greenwich Village Follies	New York, 1919
Michio Itow's Pinwheel Revel	New York, 1922
What's in a Name	New York, 1920
F. Motion Pictures	
Booloo (Paramount)	Hollywood, 1938
Madame Butterfly (Paramount)	Hollywood, 1933
No, No, Nanette (First National)	Hollywood, 1930

127

Appendix 3

DATE	THEATER	TYPE OF PERFORMANCE	ITO'S ROLE

1916 New York

DATE	THEATER	TYPE OF PERFORMANCE	ITO'S ROLE
13 Nov.	Comedy	Play: *Bushido* (Kabuki) Wash. Sq. Players	Director, choreographer, scenic director
6 Dec.	Comedy	Recital: Japanese Girl, Puccini Japanese Sword Dance Pizzicati, Delibes Shō-Jō (Spirit of Wine), Japanese melody Spirit Escaping Bondage, Saint-Saëns Marionette	Choreographer, dancer

DATE	THEATER	TYPE OF PERFORMANCE	ITO'S ROLE
1917 New York			

7 March	Comedy	Recital:
		    Female Demon,
		      Japanese melody
		    Fox, Michio Ito
		    Golliwogg's Cakewalk,
		      Debussy
		    To Odori, Japanese melody
			Choreographer, dancer

20 Aug.–3 Sept.	Booth	Ballet Intime:
		    Sakura-Sakura,
		      Japanese melody,
		      arr. by Griffes
		    Sho-Jo, Griffes
			Choreographer, dancer

Atlantic City			
5 Aug.			
Washington			
9 Aug.	Belasco		
1918 New York			

3 Feb.
 10, 17 Feb.
	Greenwich Village (not known how much was repeated)	Recital:
		    Bird Dance, Cyril Scott
		    Dō-Jō-Ji, Japanese melody
		    Echigo-Jishi,
		      Japanese melody,
		      arr. by Spier
		    Chinese Dance, A Fable
		      Tchaikovsky
		    Genroku Hanamiodori,
		      Sawada
			Choreographer, dancer

DATE	THEATER	TYPE OF PERFORMANCE	ITO'S ROLE
		Matsu-no-Midori, Japanese melody, arr. by Spier	
		Odori, Japanese melody	
		The Donkey, mime play by Michio Ito; music by Spier, piano acc. by Spier	Author, director
23–24 Feb., 2–3, 9–10 March	Neighborhood Playhouse	Play: *Tamura* (Noh trans. by Fenollosa-Pound)	Director, choreographer, actor-dancer
22 Feb.	MacDowell Club	Griffes Recital: Sho-Jo, Griffes; 5 settings of Chinese lyrics, Griffes; Griffes at piano	Choreographer, dancer
7, 14, 21 April	Greenwich Village	Recital: White Peacock, Griffes; Griffes at piano Blue Flame, Yamada Fukagawa Bushi, Yamada Kappore, Yamada Kyō-no-Shiki, Yamada Chidori no Kyoku, Yamada Tsuru Kame, Yamada Yari no Odori, Yamada (all with Yamada as accompanist) Sword Dance (Kembu), to chant Wild Men's Dance, Ornstein; acc. by Ornstein	Choreographer, dancer

DATE	THEATER	TYPE OF PERFORMANCE	ITO'S ROLE
10 July	Greenwich Village	Play: *At the Hawk's Well,* Yeats; music composed and conducted by Yamada	Director, choreographer, dancer
Washington and East Coast			
17–27 Aug.		Play and recital: Musicians Yamada and Griffes	
1919 New York			
15 July	Greenwich Village	Revue: *Greenwich Village Follies*	Choreographer, dancer, set designer
13 Oct.	Garrick	Play: *The Faithful*	Choreographer, technical directo
1920 New York			
19 March	Maxine Elliott	Revue: *What's in a Name*	Choreographer, scenic director
1921 New York			
6 Jan.	Neighborhood Playhouse	Play: *Tamura* (new production)	Director, actor-dancer, scenic director
22–23 June	Princess	Recital: Bullfighter, Albéniz Chinese Buffoon Siamese Dance, Ito Song of India, Scott	Choreographer, dancer

DATE		THEATER	TYPE OF PERFORMANCE	ITO'S ROLE
1922	**New York**			
	15 June	Earl Carroll	Revue:	Director
			Pinwheel Revel	Choreographer,
			Ecclesiastique,	scenic director,
			Schumann	dancer
	31 July	The Little	Revue:	Director,
			Michio Ito's Pinwheel	choreographer,
			Revel (new version)	scenic director,
			Jazz and Jazz	dancer
			Tropical Night	
1923	**New York**			
	? Jan.	?	Play:	Translator,
			The Fox's Grave	director,
			(Kyōgen)	actor-dancer
			She Who Was Fished	
			(Kyōgen)	
	11 March	Broadhurst	Recital:	Choreographer,
			Blue Waves	dancer
			Gavotte, Bach	
			Japanese Spear	
			Acc. by Armand Vecsey's	
			orchestra	
1925	**New York**			
	20 Oct.	National	Play:	Choreographer
			Arabesque	
1926	**New York**			
	25 Jan.	Guild	Play:	Choreographer
			Goat Song	

DATE	THEATER	TYPE OF PERFORMANCE	ITO'S ROLE
?	?	Play: *Sister Beatrice*	Choreographer, scene designe

1927   New York

DATE	THEATER	TYPE OF PERFORMANCE	ITO'S ROLE
28 March	Forty-fourth St.	Operetta: *Cherry Blossoms*	Choreographer
15 May	Times Square	Recital: Blue Boy Hymn to the Sun, Rimsky-Korsakov Sarabande, Couperin Passepied, Delibes La Joyeuse, Rameau Caresse, Scriabin Prelude no. 10, Scriabin Chinese Spear (?) Pair of Fans, Yamada Musical acc.: Yasha Bunchuck, cellist; Louis Horst, pianist; Lawrence Harp Quartet	Choreographer, dancer, costume and scene designe
18 Sept.	Royale	Operetta: *The Mikado*	Choreographer
13 Nov.	John Golden	Recital: Tango, Albéniz Chinese #1, Ravel Chinese #2, Ravel Preludes 5, 8, 6, 9, Scriabin op. 11	Choreographer, dancer

134

DATE	THEATER	TYPE OF PERFORMANCE	ITO'S ROLE
		Single Fan, Yamada Mus. acc.: Vertchamp String Quartet; Genevieve Pitot, pianist	

Washington

13 Dec.

1928 New York

11 Jan. Gallo

		Opera: *Madame Butterfly*	Choreographer, dramatic director
5 Feb.	John Golden	Recital: Valse, Chopin Ball, Chopin Warrior, Rachmaninoff Joy, Schumann Lotus Land, Scott Faun, Yamada Spring Rain, Yamada Tone Poems 1, 2, Yamada Ecclesiastique no. 2, Tchaikovsky	Choreographer, dancer

1928 New York

18 March	John Golden	Recital: Malagueña, Albéniz Burmese, Ito Javanese, Kelley Pavane, anon. Polka, Smetana	Choreographer, dancer

135

DATE	THEATER	TYPE OF PERFORMANCE	ITO'S ROLE
25 March	Jolson (now Century)	Pantomime-Play-Dance: *The Story of the Soldier.* Music by Stravinsky; book by C. S. Ramuz; orch. cond. by Pierre Monteux	Choreographer, director of drama and pantomime and dance
4, 5, 6 May	Manhattan Opera House	Performance by Neighborhood Playhouse Group: Nuages et Fêtes, Debussy	Dancer choreographer
2 Dec.	Civic Repertory	Recital: Mandarin Ducks Arabesque no. 2, Debussy Little Shepherdess, Debussy Portuguese Dance, Font y de Anta Down South, Middleton Persian, Ito Sari Dance, Hindu melody Warrior, Schumann Piano acc. by Raymond Sachse and Manuel Bernard	Choreographer

1929 New York

11 Jan.	Manhattan Opera House	Play: *Turandot*, Carlo Gozzi	Choreographer

Los Angeles

28 April	Figueroa Playhouse	Recital: Shadow, Debussy Habanera, Sarasate	Choreographer, dancer

136

DATE	THEATER	TYPE OF PERFORMANCE	ITO'S ROLE
July	Barnsdall Park Patio Theater	Recital: Spanish Fan, Sarasate Piano acc. by Raymond Sachse	Choreographer, dancer

Eagle Rock

DATE	THEATER	TYPE OF PERFORMANCE	ITO'S ROLE
5 Aug.	Argus Bowl	Recital: Somebody Nothing Kyōgen)	Choreographer, dancer, translator, director
12 Aug.	Argus Bowl	Recital: Mermaid, Debussy Ladybug, Chopin En Bateau, Debussy	Choreographer, dancer

1929 Eagle Rock

DATE	THEATER	TYPE OF PERFORMANCE	ITO'S ROLE
19 Aug.	Argus Bowl	Recital: Étude op. 10 no. 9 (F minor), Chopin Sarabande, Lully	Choreographer, dancer
26 Aug.	Argus Bowl	Recital	Choreographer, dancer
2 Sept.	Argus Bowl	Recital	Choreographer, dancer

Pasadena

DATE	THEATER	TYPE OF PERFORMANCE	ITO'S ROLE
20 Sept.	Rose Bowl	Pageant of Lights (180 dancers in symphonic dance compositions): New World Symphony, Dvorak	Choreographer, director

DATE	THEATER	TYPE OF PERFORMANCE	ITO'S ROLE
		Peer Gynt Suite, Grieg	
		Andante Cantabile, Tchaikovsky	
		Waltz in E-flat, Chopin	
		Waltz in C-sharp minor, Chopin	
		Hollywood Symphony Orchestra, cond. by Modest Altschuler	
Los Angeles			
4 Oct.	Koyasan Betsuin Hall	Recital: Piano acc. by Maude Howard and Raymond Sachse	Choreographer, dancer
5 Oct.	Koyasan Betsuin Hall	Recital: Caucasian Dance, Ippolitov-Ivanov	Choreographer, dancer
1930 Los Angeles			
10–16 Feb.	Figueroa Playhouse	*Samurai* and *Geisha* (plays by Tsutsui Company of 30)	Adapter, director
New York			
4 May	Booth		
Los Angeles			
26 Feb.	First National Studio	Film: *No, No, Nanette* (Japanese sequence)	Choreographer, director

138

DATE	THEATER	TYPE OF PERFORMANCE	ITO'S ROLE
15 Aug.	Hollywood Bowl	Symphonic dance composition with 125 dancers in Polovetski dances from Prince Igor (Los Angeles Philharmonic Orchestra conducted by Bernardino Molinari)	Choreographer, director

1931 Los Angeles

DATE	THEATER	TYPE OF PERFORMANCE	ITO'S ROLE
6 March	Philharmonic Auditorium (also played at Pasadena and San Diego)	Recital: Ecclesiastique IV, Tchaikovsky (13 dancers) Friendship, Schumann Tragedy, Schumann Cortège, Debussy Birth of a Soul, Harling Mary Magdalene, ballet pastorale comp. for Ito by W. Franke Harling (18 dancers, 4 singers, orch, cond. by Harling, piano acc. by Raymond Sachse)	Choreographer, director, dancer

1932 Los Angeles

DATE	THEATER	TYPE OF PERFORMANCE	ITO'S ROLE
15 Jan.	Wilshire Ebell	Kabuki: Japanese Children's Theater	Adapter, director, producer
Aug.	Weller Street	Japanese Spring Dance (part of Olympic Games celebration), Japanese orchestra	Choreographer, director

139

DATE	THEATER	TYPE OF PERFORMANCE	ITO'S ROLE
1933 **Los Angeles**			
5 Jan.	Paramount Studio	Motion Picture: *Madame Butterfly*	Choreographer, director
25 Aug.	Greek Theater, Griffith Park	Recital: Sonata, Beethoven Minuet, Boccherini Clair de Lune, Debussy Cortège du Sardar, Ippolitov-Ivanov Dancing Girl, Scott Gnossienne no. 1, Satie Greek Theater Symphony Orchestra cond. by Leonard Walker	Choreographer
1935 **Los Angeles**			
26 May	Southern California Japanese School Association	Recital: Harlequin and Columbine, Beethoven, Piano acc. by Carol Van Alstyne	Choreographer, dancer
1936 **Los Angeles**			
17 June	Wilshire Ebell	Recital: Minuet, Debussy Gnossienne no 2, Satie	Choreographer, dancer
Redlands			
26 June	Redlands Bowl	Opera: *Orpheus*, Gluck (35 dancers interpreting stage action)	Choreographer, dramatic director

DATE		THEATER	TYPE OF PERFORMANCE	ITO'S ROLE
	Los Angeles			
	25 Oct.	Philharmonic Auditorium	Opera: *La Traviata*	Choreographer, dance director
1937	*Los Angeles*			
	19 Aug.	Hollywood Bowl	Symphonic dance compositions: *Etenraku* (23 dancers) *Blue Danube*, Strauss (54 dancers) Los Angeles Philharmonic Orchestra cond. by Hidemaro Konoye	Choreographer, director
1937	*Los Angeles*			
	24 Sept.	Hollywood Bowl	Symphonic dance compositions: Two Menuettos, Mozart (32 dancers) Little Symphony Orchestra cond. by Adolf Tandler	Choreographer, director
	20 Nov.	Polytechnic Auditorium	Recital: Maid with Flaxen Hair, Debussy	Choreographer
1938	*Los Angeles*			
	22 July	Paramount Studio	Film: *Booloo*	Actor, technical director
1941	*Los Angeles*			
	8 Nov.	Koyasan Betsuin Hall	Dance recital of Teiko Ito	Director, choreographer

Appendix 4

The basis of Michio Ito's dances was ten arm movements, which he called the "Ten Gestures." These gestures have two forms, which he termed "A" and "B" or "masculine" and "feminine." Although the conclusion of each gesture is indicated by a given number, the gesture itself is, properly speaking, the *whole movement* of that gesture. The photographs that follow illustrate the ten gestures in their "A" aspect.*

A gesture may start from any point required by the idea and the context of the dance; likewise it may move into any other gesture that may be desired. For simplicity's sake, however, the movement represented below goes along the path followed by a regular progression, both hands in unison, from the conclusion of 10A → 1A → 2A → 3A → 4A → 5A → 6A → 7A → 8A → 9A → 10A.

In the dances, of course, there is no such regular progression. One hand may be performing one gesture, the other a different one. Each gesture may evolve from any other, moving backward or forward; that is, one may move from 1A to 10A as well as from 10A to 1A, from 2A to 4B or,

143

*These photographs (pp. 144-153) were reproduced from old 16 mm. color motion picture film.

vice versa, from 4B to 2A, and so on. The angle of hand and arm to the body will vary, as will also the turn of the wrist, the ancillary movements of head, shoulders, legs, and feet, as well as the rhythm, tempo, and attack employed for each movement—all under the strict control of the dancer's mind.

When one considers these and other possible combinations and alterations, one can perhaps conceive of the variety that exists in Ito's dance compositions, both within a single dance and among the many dances. What one cannot conceive of is the breathtaking strength and beauty created by each dance; that has to be seen.

10

1

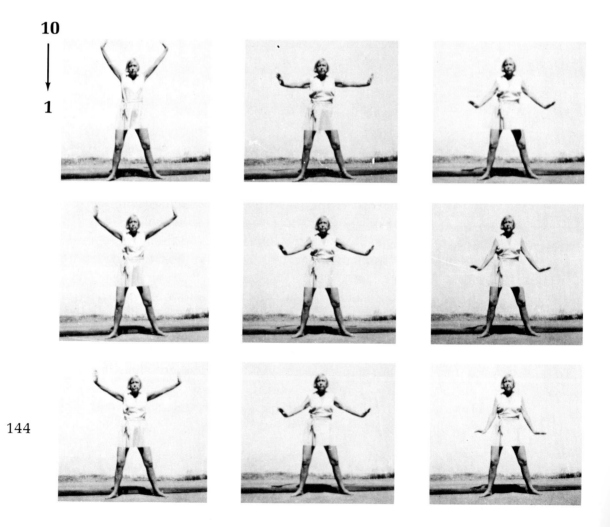

144

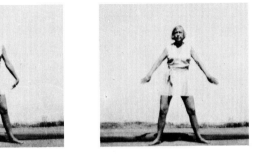

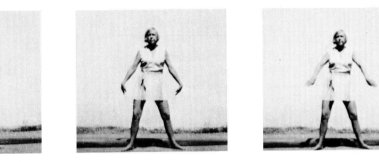

1

2

2

↓

3

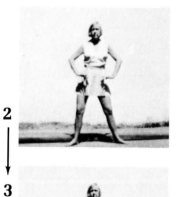

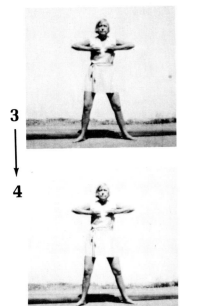

3

4

4

5

147

 **5**

 **6**

148

6

↓

7

149

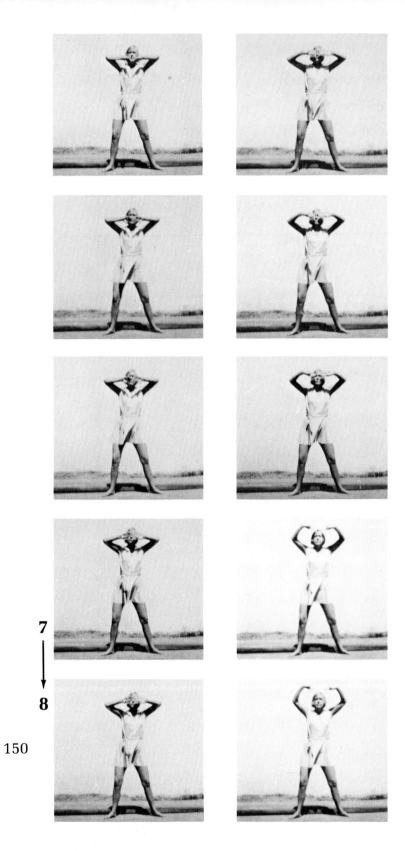

8

↓

9

7

↓

8

150

151

9

152

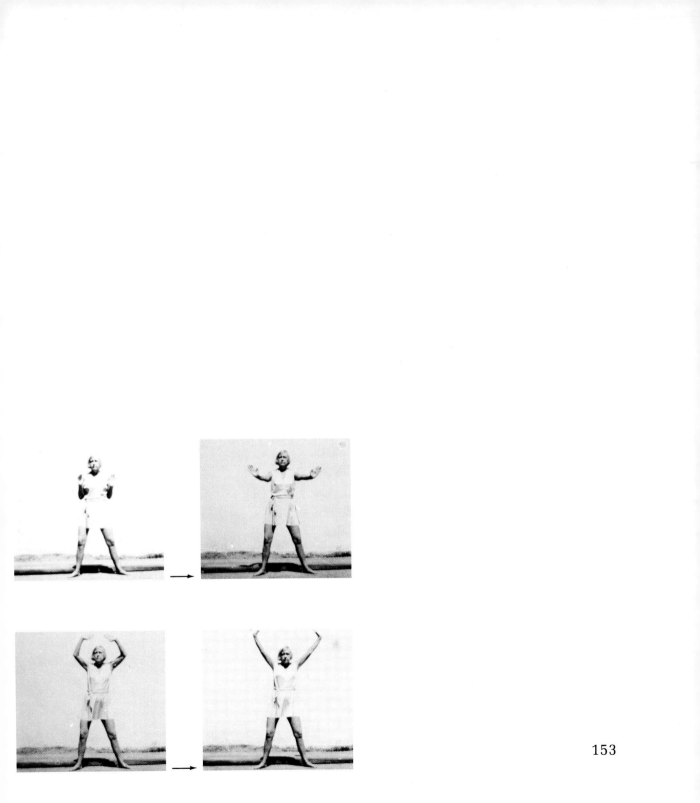

153

Notes

I. The Dance Poems of Michio Ito

1. I can perform and have notes on, or film record of, these solo dances; perhaps other pupils of Ito's retain some knowledge of his dances. I have incomplete notes on two of his symphonic choreographies.

2. Cf. the ball game "as symbolic working out of man's struggle to master his fate" (Irene Nicholson, "Mexican and Central American Mythology," in Cottie Burland, Irene Nicholson, and Harold Osborne, *Mythology of the Americas* [London: Hamlyn, 1970], pp. 245-246). Nickolas Muray (in *Dance Magazine* [May 1928], p. 38) mentions discussion among spectators at the first performance of this dance and his belief that it "was an abstract interpretation of the carefreeness of youth, the play with the imaginary ball representing Time which once thrown away never comes back"—an erroneous impression which subsequent viewings would no doubt have corrected. The "imaginary" ball is returned each time, and, although with his final gesture the dancer tosses it again, there is no assurance that he will not receive it again (see p. 5, above).

The original title of *Ball* was *Atlanta*, perhaps referring to America on the shores of the Atlantic, where baseball is supposed to have originated and where Michio Ito attended the game that inspired his dance.

3. Laurence Binyon, *The Flight of the Dragon: An Essay on the Theory and Practice of Art in China and Japan Based on Original Sources* (New York: Grove Press, 1961), pp. 64-65.

4. Émile Jaques-Dalcroze, *Rhythm, Music and Education*, trans. Harold F. Rubinstein (New York and London: Putnam, 1921), p. 244; see also pp. 232, 296, 297-298.

5. Archibald MacLeish, *Poetry and Experience* (Baltimore: Penguin Books, 1964), p. 169.

6. Laurence Binyon, *Painting in the Far East*, 3d ed. (New York: Dover, 1959), p. 158.

7. Machado de Assis, *Esau and Jacob*, trans. Helen Caldwell (Berkeley and Los Angeles: University of California Press, 1965), p. 99.

8. Faubion Bowers, *Scriabin*, 2 vols. (Tokyo and Palo Alto: Kodansha International, 1969), I, 240-241.

9. Alfred J. Swan, *Scriabin* (London: John Lane and Bodley Head, 1969), pp. 72-73.

10. The butterfly, symbol of resurrection, is particularly appropriate in this dance.

11. Bowers, *Scriabin*, II, 54.

12. W. B. Yeats, *Essays and Introductions* (New York: Macmillan, 1961), p. 216.

13. Arthur Machen, *Hieroglyphics*, Caerleon ed. (London: Martin Secker, 1923), chap. 3, p. 73.

14. George Santayana, *Three Philosophical Poets* (Garden City, N.Y.: Doubleday, Anchor Books, 1938), pp. 19-20.

15. John Unterecker, *A Reader's Guide to William Butler Yeats* (New York: Farrar, Straus, Noonday Press, 1959), p. 32.

16. Yeats, *Essays and Introductions*, pp. 522, 509; cf. p. 352: "Works of art are always begotten by previous works of art."

17. Binyon, *Painting*, p. 123.

18. Jean Chevalier, *Dictionnaire des Symboles* (Paris: Robert Laffont, [1969]), s.v. "Eventail."

19. Frederick H. Martens, in a prefatory note to Kosçak Yamada, *Three Old Japanese Art Dances for Piano Solo* (New York: Carl Fischer, 1919). See also Daiji Maruoka and Tatsuo Yoshikoshi, *Noh*, trans. Don Kenny (Osaka: Hoikusha, 1969), pp. 5, 12; Gaston Renondeau, *Nô* (Tokyo: Maison Franco-Japonaise, 1953), pp. 205-215; Chevalier, *Dictionnaire*, s.v. "Tortue," "Grue."

20. Ovid *Metamorphoses* VIII 618-724.

21. By Zeami (1363-1444), originally entitled *Aioi no Matsu* ("The Pair of Pine Trees Grown Together"), in *Japanese Noh Drama*, vol. 1: *Ten Plays Selected and Translated from the Japanese* (Tokyo: Nippon Gakujutsu Shinkoka, 1955), pp. 1-17; *Introduction to Classic Japanese Literature*, ed. and pub. Kokusai Bunka Shinkokai (Tokyo, 1948), pp. 145-148; Maruoka and Yoshikoshi, *Noh*, pp. 8-9; Chevalier, *Dictionnaire*, s.v. "Pin."

22. Lewis Bush, *Japanalia*, 5th ed. (New York: David McKay, 1959), s.v. "Jō To Uba."

23. Homer *Odyssey* IX 82-104.

24. Chevalier, *Dictionnaire*, s.v. "Apsara."

25. Ibid., s.v. "Lotus"; Binyon, *Painting*, p. 129.

26. Binyon, *Painting*, p. 130; Emma Hawkridge, *Indian Gods and Kings* (Boston and New York: Houghton Mifflin, 1935), pp. 44-46.

27. Binyon, *Painting*, p. 70.

28. Yeats, "Certain Noble Plays of Japan," in *Essays and Introductions*, p. 224.

29. Franz Liszt, *F. Chopin* (Leipzig: Breitkopf and Haertel, 1879), p. 111.

30. On this étude (F minor, op. 10 no. 9) see Herbert Weinstock, *Chopin: The Man and His Music* (New York: Knopf, 1949), pp. 193-194.

31. Golliwogg first appears in Bertha Upton, *The Adventures of Two Dutch Dolls*, pictures by Florence K. Upton (London: Longmans Green, n.d.). His further adventures are told in numerous "Golliwogg" books by the same author and illustrator.

32. In *The Golliwogg at the Seaside* (1898).

33. Plato *Laws* II 654a.

34. Dylan Thomas, Vol. III, Reading "A Few Words of a Kind" (New York: Caedmon Records, 1953), TC-1043A; cf. Yeats, *Essays and Introductions*, p. 523. Cf. T. S. Eliot: "The first [function of poetry] is that poetry has to give pleasure" (*On Poetry and Poets* [London: Faber and Faber, 1957], p. 18).

35. Anthony Burgess, "Speaking of Books: the Writer's Purpose," *New York Times Book Review*, 1 May 1966, pp. 1, 43.

36. Israel Shenker, "Helen Gardner" (an interview), *New York Times*, 7 June 1973, p. 56.

37. William Wordsworth, preface to "Lyrical Ballads" (1800); cf. MacLeish, *Poetry and Experience*, pp. 70-71.

38. Yeats, *Essays and Introductions*, pp. 287, 339.

39. Binyon, *Flight of the Dragon*, p. 6.

40. Binyon, *Painting*, pp. 23-24.

41. Binyon, *Flight of the Dragon*, p. 16.

42. Binyon, *Painting*, p. 62.

43. Burgess, "Speaking of Books."

44. Helen Caldwell, "Ito and Herodotus," *UCLAN Review* (Winter 1964), pp. 13,14.

45. Ibid., p. 14.

46. Ibid.

47. Ito's ten gestures had two forms, which he termed "A" and "B" or "masculine" and "feminine" or "objective" and "subjective." He was influenced in this systemization by Dalcroze, whose school at Hellerau he attended in 1912-1914.

48. Binyon, *Flight of the Dragon*, p. 60; cf. Frayne Williams, "Theater Production," lecture at University of California, Los Angeles, 12 January 1928: "The public always prefers spectacle to drama; and if you give them what they want you will become bankrupt before sating their ever-growing expectation." That is, spectacle leaves the gray matter and the emotions undisturbed; it is not art but merely entertainment.

49. Dylan Thomas recording; see n. 34, above.

50. Binyon, *Painting*, p. 274.

51. Duke Ellington, "Duke Ellington, *Sine Qua Non*," *Esquire* (June 1973), p. 178.

II. "At the Hawk's Well"

1. Ito, with obvious symbolism, used this expression as the subtitle for his "Memories" of his beginnings as a dancer: "Omoide o Katuru: Takanoya" ["Memories of Things Past: Hawk's Well"], *Hikaku Bunka*, II (Tokyo, 1956), 57-76.

2. *Ibid.*

3. The Coliseum on St. Martin's Lane, almost opposite the Duke of York's Theatre, was opened in 1904 as London's most modern and luxurious theater. It is still London's largest theater but is no longer a variety house; since 1931 it has been used for musical comedies and spectaculars. Before and during World War I such celebrities as Sarah Bernhardt, Réjane, Ellen Terry, Mary Anderson, Lillah McCarthy, and the Abbey players appeared on its stage. See Felix Barker, *The House That Stoll Built: The Story of the Coliseum Theatre* (London: Frederick Muller, 1957); Raymond Mander and Joe Mitchenson, *The Theatres of London* (London: R. Hart-Davis, 1961), pp. 41-46; William Kent, *An Encyclopedia of London* (London: Dent, 1970), p. 378.

4. *Times* (London), 11 May 1915, p. 6.

5. The biographic material was obtained from Michio Ito himself, from his "Memories" (cited in n. 1), and from periodicals cited in nn. 6, 7, and 8. Ito's birth date is usually given as 13 April 1893 (see, for example, *Dai Jimmei Jiten*, ed. Yasaburo Shimonaka [Tokyo: Heibonsha, 1958], IX, 80; *Japan Biographical Encyclopedia and Who's Who*, 3d ed., 1964-1965 [Tokyo: Rengo Press], p. 2242; obituary, *New York Times*, 7 November 1961). But it would seem, from his "Memories" and other interviews, that the year was more likely 1892 or 1891. The inconsistencies perhaps arose in transposing from the Japanese system of reckoning dates by government administrations.

6. *Theatre Magazine* (New York) (Sept. 1927), p. 39.

7. *L'Echo de Paris*, 9 June 1911, p. 4.

8. Eurythmics was originated by Émile Jaques-Dalcroze (1865-1950). Brief descriptions of the system, the institute at Hellerau, and its festivals may be found in Walther R. Volbach, *Adolphe Appia, a Prophet of the Modern Theatre: A Profile* (Middletown, Conn.: Wesleyan University Press, 1968), pp. 82-89; Adolphe Appia, *The Work of Living Art: A Theory of the Theatre*, trans. with introd. by H. D. Albright (Coral Gables: University of Miami Press, 1960), pp. xv. xvi, 8-9. For more extensive discussion see Émile Jaques-Dalcroze, *Rhythm, Music and Education*, trans. Harold F. Rubinstein (New York and London: Putnam, 1921); Dalcroze, *Eurythmics, Art and Education*, trans. Frederick Rothwell (London: Chatto and Windus, 1930); Jo Pennington, *The Importance of Being Rhythmic* (New York and London: Putnam, 1925). See also *George Bernard Shaw and Mrs. Patrick Campbell: Their Correspondence*, ed. Alan Dent (New York: Knopf, 1952), pp. 137-140; Paul Claudel, "La Séduction d'Hellerau," in *Mes Idées sur le Théâtre* ([Paris]: Gallimard, 1966), pp. 40-46; see also chap. iii, n. 5, below.

9. In the Kabuki company attached to the Imperial Theater and in the Hanayagi school. See *New York Times*, 21 Aug. 1917, p. 7; *New York Tribune*, 19 Aug. 1917, Sec. IV, p. 2; 14 July 1918, Sec. IV, p. 2; 26 Oct. 1919, Sec. IV, p. 6; Komiya Toyotaka, *Japanese Music and Drama in the Meiji Era*, trans. Edward G. Seidensicker and Donald Keene (Tokyo: Obunsha, 1956) pp. 256-259; Zoë Kincaid, *Kabuki: The Popular Stage of Japan* (London: Macmillan, 1925), pp. 353, 367-368.

Ito
with miniature
Noh masks
given him by
his father,
the architect
and art collector
Tamekichi Ito
1931
Photograph
by Toyo Miyatake

"The samurai wisdom and sweetness that come from self-conquest"
(see page 17). Ito in Japanese armor London 1915. *"When I first put
on my grandfather's armor my grandmother cried, because I was so
like my grandfather at eighteen,"* Ezra Pound quoting Ito in the
Fortnightly Review. *Photograph by Alvin Langdon Coburn*

10. ——— Maeda; Gorō Soganoya (1877-1948), famous comedian and writer of comic sketches (*Japan Biographical Encyclopedia*); Aoi Ikuta, novelist and playwright (*Dai Jimmei Jiten*).

11. Tsuguharu Foujita, also spelled Tsugui Fujita (1886-1968), spent most of his life in France and was famous for his paintings of cats (*Japan Biographical Encyclopedia*, s.v. "Fujita, Tsugui"; *Dictionnaire Biographique Français Contemporain*, 2d ed., 1954-1955 [Paris: Agence Internationale de Documentation Contemporaine, n.d.], s.v. "Foujita, Tsuguharu"). Foujita and his wife visited Ito in 1935 in Hollywood.

12. Kanai Yamamoto (1882-1946) was a Tokyo painter (*Japan Biographical Encyclopedia*, s.v. "Yamamoto, Kanai").

13. Besides Ito's "Memories," see *New York Tribune*, 14 July 1918, Sec. IV, p. 2. Perhaps the word "parties" should be explained. A party to Michio Ito was any social gathering from a simple lunch of two persons in a modest restaurant to an extravagant blowout involving many. The parties he mentions here were probably lunches and dinners at the Café Royal.

14. For Lady Ottoline Morrell as art patron see William Rothenstein, *Men and Memories: A History of the Arts, 1872-1922, Being the Recollections of William Rothenstein*, 2 vols. in 1 (New York: Tudor, n.d.), II, 96; see also pp. 89, 172-173, 213.

15. Henry Wood (1869-1944), conductor of the Queen's Hall Orchestra.

16. Shaw at this time asked Ito what he was doing in England; Ito replied that he was studying art. Later, when Ito had attained fame with his dancing, Shaw asked him the same question and Ito gave the same answer, whereupon Shaw smiled approvingly.

17. Maude Alice Burke, an American born in San Francisco, was married to Sir Bache Cunard (of the steamship line) (see Daphne Fielding, *Those Remarkable Cunards, Emerald and Nancy: Lady Cunard and Her Daugher* [New York: Athenaeum, 1968]).

18. Canto 77.

19. In his "Memories" Ito states that this pastime became a bore.

20. For example, Ito is reported to have practiced in Ezra Pound's flat as Carl Dolmetesch accompanied him on the clavichord (Charles Norman, *Ezra Pound*, rev. ed. [New York: Funk and Wagnalls, 1969], p. 183).

21. *Ottoline: The Early Memoirs of Lady Ottoline Morrell*, ed. Robert Gathorne-Hardy (London: Faber and Faber, 1964), pp. 276-282. The "painter" Guevara was Alvaro Guevara, a Chilean born in Spain. He is briefly described in Fielding, *Emerald and Nancy*, pp. 52-53, with his picture facing p. 53 and his portrait of Nancy facing p. 78.

22. *New York Tribune*, 19 Aug. 1917, Sec. IV, p. 2.

23. *Hangman's House* (New York and London: Century, 1926), pp. 123-126.

24. "Memories." Cf. Lady Ottoline's comment (June 1915): "The Japanese dancer Ito was the next visitor. This quiet little figure who seemed as if he had emerged out of an old Japanese print put himself back into one here. For he spent his days fishing in one of the ponds under blossoming quince and apple trees, while Maria Nys [later to marry Aldous Huxley] in a white dress flitted round about him with

adoring eyes" (*Ottoline at Garsington: Memoirs of Lady Ottoline Morrell, 1915-1918*, ed. Robert Gathorne-Hardy (London: Faber and Faber, 1974), p. 41.

25. "Memories."

26. According to Noel Stock, *The Life of Ezra Pound* (London: Routledge and Kegan Paul, 1970), p. 148, Pound received the first Fenollosa material from Mrs. Fenollosa toward the end of 1913 and in November 1915 she sent a further packet from Alabama. Cf. Hugh Kenner, *The Pound Era* (Berkeley, Los Angeles, London: University of California Press, 1971), p. 198; *The Letters of Ezra Pound, 1907-1941*, ed. D. D. Paige, 1st ed. (New York: Harcourt, Brace, 1950), #36, London, 31 Jan. 1914, to Harriet Monroe. D. J. Gordon and Ian Fletcher, in "The Poet and the Theatre," in *W. B. Yeats: Images of a Poet* (Manchester: Manchester University Press, 1961), p. 62, give 1912 as the year Pound received the Fenollosa manuscripts.

27. Ito, "Memories."

28. *Visions and Beliefs in the West of Ireland*, coll. and arr. by Lady Gregory, with two essays and notes by W. B. Yeats (Gerrards Cross: Colin Smythe, 1970), p. 333, note signed W. B. Y., 14 Oct. 1914: "Last winter Mr. Ezra Pound was editing the late Professor Fenollosa's translations of the Noh Drama of Japan and read me a great deal of what he was doing." Cf. Pound's letter to Harriet Monroe (see n. 26): "You'll find W. B. Y. also very keen on it [i.e., his translation of Noh]."

29. Ezra Pound, "Study of Noh Continues in West," *Japan Times* (Tokyo), 10 Dec. 1939, p. 8.

30. Curtis B. Bradford, *Yeats at Work* (Carbondale and Edwardsville: Southern Illinois University Press, 1965), pp. 174-175; *Letters of Ezra Pound*, #84, London, 9 March 1916, to Kate Buss: "Yeats is making a new start on the foundation of these Noh dramas"; William Butler Yeats, *Letters*, ed. Allan Wade (London: R. Hart-Davis, 1954), Wade's introduction to Pt. IV, 1909-1917, pp. 520-521; Earl Miner, *The Japanese Tradition in British and American Literature* (Princeton: Princeton University Press, 1958), p. 244.

31. See p. 50, below. Cf. Yeats, *Letters*, 24 Aug. 1929, to Olivia Shakespear: "Everyone here is as convinced as I am that I have discovered a new form by this combination of dance, speech and music."

32. Bradford, *Yeats at Work*, pp. 174-211; *Letters of Ezra Pound*, #84, 9 March 1916: "My occupations this week consist in ... bother a good deal about the production of Yeats' new play."

33. Ito, "Memories"; cf. Bradford, *Yeats at Work*, p. 171: "Between 1910 and 1916 Yeats wrote no new plays."

34. This date jibes with Yeats's references to working on a new play. He wrote to Robert Bridges on 1 Aug. 1915 (Yeats, *Letters*, p. 599): "I shall be here till September I imagine. It is my one chance of finishing a new play"; and on 26 September to Ernest Boyd: "Forgive my not having written but I have been wrapped up in a new play."

35. Ito, "Memories." Ito's opinion that Noh was "the damnedest thing in this world" may have been formed at the time his schoolmates Kume and Kayano were studying it, perhaps making fun of their instruction and practice. Schoolboys being what they are, and Michio Ito's spirit of fun being what it was, there is little doubt that he too "performed" Noh in his way, mimicking his friends' attempts. In 1930 he gave a very good imitation for my benefit when I expressed enthusiasm over a Noh performance I had just attended.

36. Pound, "Study of Noh Continues," p. 8.

37. Ito, "Memories." In the same way, Yeats quite clearly appreciated Ito's dancing (see, for example, p. 53, above). Ezra Pound, as surely, did not quite understand it although he expressed admiration both for Ito and his dancing; e.g., in "Remy de Gourmont," *Fortnightly Review* (1 Dec. 1915), p. 1165, Pound illustrates Ito's poetic ability. See also *Letters of Ezra Pound*, #369, 22 Jan. 1940, to Katue Kitasono, and #74, 25 Sept. 1915 (sic), to Harriet Monroe. In the latter Pound compares Ito's dancing with the Russian ballet, with which it had no relation.

38. Ito, "Memories"; Janet Leeper, *Edward Gordon Craig Designs for the Theatre* (Harmsworth: Penguin Books, 1948), p. 46, note by Craig.

39. Edward Gordon Craig, *The Theatre Advancing* (Boston: Little, Brown, 1919), p. 105.

40. *Letters of Ezra Pound*, #326, April 1937, to John Lackay Brown: "If Yeats knew a fugue from a frog . . ."; cf. his letter on Yeats's reading Burns, #189, Paris, 9 July 1922, to Felix E. Schelling. Yeats, for his part, although he appreciated Pound's understanding of musical reading, regarded his singing as "like something on a very bad phonograph" (Yeats, *Letters*, p. 543, 10 Dec. 1909, to Lady Gregory).

41. A. Norman Jeffares, *W. B. Yeats, Man and Poet* (New York: Barnes and Noble, 1966), p. 165; Gerald Moore, "The Noh and the Dance Plays of W. B. Yeats," *Japan Quarterly*, VII (April-June 1960), 184; Anthony Thwaite, "Yeats and the Noh," *Twentieth Century* (Sept. 1957), p. 237; Walter Starkie, "Yeats and the Abbey Theatre," in *Homage to Yeats, 1865-1965: Papers Read at a Clark Library Seminar, October 16, 1965*, by Walter Starkie and A. Norman Jeffares (Los Angeles: University of California William Andrew Clark Memorial Library, 1966), pp. 28-29.

42. Ito, "Memories"; cf. Thwaite, "Yeats and the Noh," p. 237.

43. A. C. Scott, *The Kabuki Theatre of Japan* (London: Allen and Unwin, 1955), pp. 35, 75, 88-89, 91-97, 100, 101, 103, and passim; cf. Shūtarō Miyake, *Kabuki Drama* (Tokyo: Japan Travel Bureau, 1964), pp. 16, 92, 113, 141, 143-144.

44. See illustrations, pp. 46, 47, 80-81.

45. I watched Ito teach this dance to Lester Horton for the 1929 performances at Eagle Rock; for the general effect see John Rees Moore, *Masks of Love and Death: Yeats as Dramatist* (Ithaca and London: Cornell University Press, 1971), pp. 193-194.

46. Herodotus II 80.2 and note by Waddell, *Herodotus Book II*, ed. W. G. Waddell (London: Methuen, 1939).

47. Ito, "Memories." Ito also describes the colors of his costume: legs, red tights; front, cream and black; back, brown with gold feathers; headdress of blonde; and he adds, "we made this in Dulac's house."

48. *Times* (London), 27 March 1916, p. 11; 5 April 1916, p. 11; *Harper's Bazaar* (March 1917), p. 56.

49. Serge Sauneron, *The Priests of Egypt*, trans. Ann Morrissett (New York: Grove Press, 1960), pp. 176, 177; Jean Chevalier, *Dictionnaire des Symboles* (Paris: Laffont, [1969]), s.v. "Faucon."
The original title of the play was *The Well of Immortality* (Bradford, *Yeats at Work*, p. 175). According to Ito, Yeats associated the water in the well with "wisdom," a symbol in conformity with Orphic teachings; cf. Oliver St. John Gogarty, *It Isn't This Time of Year at All* (New York: Doubleday, 1954), p. 245.

50. See n. 32, above. There is a story—which should not be dignified with notice except that it has appeared in so many otherwise serious and scholarly books—to the effect that Ito danced outside the hawk's cage at the London zoo, "prancing," "swirling," "gyrating," and "flapping his arms" in imitation of the bird, as Yeats stood by with smiles of encouragement and a wondering crowd gathered to see the "madman." According to Joseph Hone, Yeats also danced before the amazed populace. I cannot vouch for William Butler Yeats, but so far as Michio Ito is concerned the story must be branded not only apochryphal but also utterly impossible. Ito's decorum never forsook him, and, as I have mentioned elsewhere, there was nothing of the exhibitionist in his nature; he never attracted attention to himself in any way. Further, as I have shown, he did not create dances by dancing them but rather by thinking, imagining, visualizing, meditating. We know that as a preliminary to creating his fox dance he "studied the ways of a fox"—very likely at the London zoo—and it is not impossible that he watched the hawk there. But the rest is sheer fancy; and it might be noted that of all the learned narrators listed below, Walter Starkie is the only one to quote a source for the story, namely, a friend named Harmsworth.

There is, however, a true "zoo" story in connection with *The Hawk's Well*, which Michio Ito told me in 1936; and the same story is related by J. G. Mills in "W. B. Yeats and Noh" (*Japan Quarterly*, [Oct.-Dec. 1955], p. 500). In the play appears the stage direction, "The Girl gives the cry of the hawk," and this direction is repeated. The trouble was no one knew what "the cry of the hawk" was, not even Yeats. Dulac and Ito went to the zoo to listen to the hawk, which, however, was singularly uncommunicative that day. And Dulac—Dulac, mind you, not Ito—surreptitiously poked the hawk with the tip of his umbrella. The hawk still refused to oblige, responding only with an almost inaudible peep. Later Ito and Dulac returned at feeding time, hoping the hawk would then be in better voice. The concerted screams of all the birds, however, made it impossible to distinguish which was the hawk's. The two researchers fell back on onomatopoeia to solve their problem. Perhaps the Japanese word for hawk, *taka*, was imitative of the bird's cry. Be that as it may, "taka" became "the cry of the hawk" in the play's production. This story, it is plain, is a far cry—decidedly more than a hawk's cry—from the tale of Yeats and Ito dancing among the birds at the London zoo.

Among those relating the zoo-dance story are the following: Alvin Coburn, *Alvin Langdon Coburn, Photographer: An Autobiography*, ed. Helmut and Alison Gernsheim (London: Faber and Faber, 1966), pp. 70-71; Joseph Hone, *W. B. Yeats, 1865-1939* (New York: Macmillan, 1943), pp. 308-309; Miner, *Japanese Tradition*, p. 246; Norman, *Ezra Pound*, p. 183; Starkie, "Yeats and the Abbey Theatre," pp. 29-30; F. A. C. Wilson, *Yeats's Iconography* (London: Victor Gollancz, 1960), p. 35; D. J. Gordon et al., *W. B. Yeats: Images of a Poet* (Manchester: Manchester University Press, 1961), p. 64.

51. See n. 32, above.

52. W. B. Yeats, *Four Plays for Dancers* (New York: Macmillan, 1921), pp. v-vii; Yeats, *Letters*, p. 607, n. by Wade; Coburn, *Autobiography*, p. 70.

53. Bradford, *Yeats at Work*, pp. 174-216.

54. Yeats, *Letters*, 26 March 1916, to Lady Gregory.

55. Canto 77; see also *Letters of Ezra Pound*, #369, 22 Jan. 1940, to Katue Kitasono.

56. Yeats, *Letters*, 2 April 1916, to John Quinn; 28 March, 10 April 1916, to Lady Gregory.

57. Ibid., 2 April 1916, to Quinn; 5 March 1916, to J. B. Yeats, n. by Wade, p. 607; Yeats, *Four Plays*, p. 87.

58. Yeats, *Four Plays*, p. 87.

59. Christopher Hassall, *Edward Marsh, Patron of the Arts* (London: Longmans, 1959), pp. 383-384. As to the audience not knowing which players wore masks, see also Yeats, *Letters*, 10 April 1916, to Lady Gregory.

60. Yeats, *Four Plays*, p. 87; *Times* (London), 27 March 1916, p. 11; 4 April, p. 11; 5 April, p. 11.

61. Yeats, *Four Plays*, p. 87.

62. Yeats, *Letters*, 10 April 1916, to Lady Gregory, n. by Wade, p. 611; *Four Plays*, p. 87.

63. Yeats, *Letters*, 10 April 1916, to Lady Gregory.

64. T. S. Eliot, "Ezra Pound," *Poetry* (Sept. 1946), p. 326; cf. Eliot, *On Poetry and Poets* (London: Faber and Faber, 1957), pp. 256, 260.

65. E.g., Bradford (*Yeats at Work*, p. 171): ". . . *At the Hawk's Well*; in this play for dancers Yeats invented his most characteristic and original dramatic form." See also ibid., pp. xii, 174-175; Harold Bloom, *Yeats* (New York: Oxford University Press, 1970), pp. 294, 295; Miner, *Japanese Tradition*, chap. viii.

66. W. B. Yeats, *Essays and Introductions* (New York: Macmillan, 1961), pp. 221-222.

67. Yeats, *Letters*, 2 April 1916, to Quinn.

68. Yeats, *Letters*, 28 March and 10 April 1916, to Lady Gregory.

69. Ito, "Memories." It is interesting that Yeats had decided the war would be over by 1919.

70. Yeats, *Essays and Introductions*, p. 222.

71. Ibid., pp. 224, 236.

72. Yeats, *Four Plays*, p. 88.

73. Ibid., pp. v. vi.

74. Miner, *Japanese Tradition*, pp. 245-246.

75. Ibid., pp. 240-254.

76. Yeats, *Essays and Introductions*, p. 224.

77. Yeats, *Letters*.

78. Cf. a description of a later performance of *Hawk's Well* and the effect on Yeats in Gogarty, *It Isn't This Time of Year at All*, pp. 242-247.

79. On the occasion of their parents' fiftieth wedding anniversary, the seven Ito sons (and the two daughters also, apparently) gathered together in Tokyo. The sons were all in artistic professions and one daughter was married to a painter. As part of a dance concert, Michio's translation of *Hawk's Well* was presented by five of the brothers: stage setting and masks were designed by Kisaku; Yuji composed the music and made the costumes; Osuke directed the music; Kunio (famous as an actor under the name Koreya Senda) played the Young Man; Michio, the Old Man; and Yuji's wife, Teiko, the Hawk. Only Kanaye and Teiryo, architects like their father, had no part in the production. See *Japan Times*, 26 Nov., 4 Dec. 1939; cf. *Letters of Ezra Pound*, #369, 22 Jan. 1940, to Katue Kitasono.

80. See Mills's account ("W. B. Yeats and Noh," p. 500): "He [Ito] is planning to produce a new version of *At the Hawk's Well* in Japanese this autumn in Tokyo. In his opinion Yeats' drama has a living and modern spirit which is highly suitable for a modern Noh drama and a modern stage that stresses the three-dimensional aspect. . . .

"That there is considerable interest in Yeats' *At the Hawk's Well* in Japan is also evident from the fact that the play was translated, altered and converted into an old Noh play proper by Mr. Yokomichi Mario and that it was produced in Tokyo in 1949, 1950 and 1952 on the Noh stage. . . . Mr. Kita Minoru who played the part of the old man in this production is a leader of the Kita School of the Noh." Cf. Anthony Thwaite, "Yeats and the Noh," p. 242.

III. The Artist in New York

1. *New York Tribune*, 14 July 1918, Sec. IV, p. 2.

2. *New York Times*, 7 Nov. 1961 (Michio Ito's obituary). But see Keyes Porter, "As an Oriental Looks at Art," *The Dance* (Jan. 1926), p. 35. I have in my possession Ito's prospectus for 1928, which mentions Morosco in this connection.

3. *Bushido* (the way of the samurai) is the Terakoya (school) scene by Takeda Izumo (1691-1756) from the longer work *Sugawara Denju Tenarai Kagami* (teaching of the secrets of Sugawara's calligraphy) by four playwrights at Osaka in 1746; see A. C. Scott, *The Kabuki Theatre of Japan* (London: Allen and Unwin, 1955), pp. 261-270.

4. *New York Times*, 10 June 1974, p. 32.

5. See chap. ii, n. 8, and chap. iv, nn. 11, 12; cf. Frank E. Washburn Freund, "Hellerau during 1913," *The Stage Year Book* (London), 1914, pp. 81-96; Kenneth Macgowan, *The Theatre of Tomorrow* (New York: Boni and Liveright, 1921), pp. 77-84, 190-191. For Ito's early experimentation with lights on his dances, see review (*New York Times*, 8 March 1917, p. 9): "The 'demon' was done here by Mme. Sada Yacco in full limelight years ago. Mr. Itow presented it as a harpy of shadows snatched upward by a whirlwind before the astonished eyes of the beholders."

6. Michio Ito, "Omoide o Kataru: Takanoya" ("Memories of Things Past: Hawk's Well"), *Hikaku Bunka*, II (Tokyo, 1956), 57-76.

7. Ibid. Ito had made elaborate notes and sketches for the production, a practice that he followed later, at least for the symphonic choreographies; see chap. iv, n. 17.

8. Cf. Edward M. Maisel on musical criticism's "lowering of artistic standards [in 1918] to a level even beneath what it had been in normal times" (*Charles T. Griffes: The Life of an American Composer* (New York: Knopf, 1943), p. 218. Cf. comments on the mental density of New York critics toward Copeau's work in Walther R. Volbach, *Adolphe Appia, a Prophet of the Modern Theatre: A Profile* (Middletown, Conn.: Wesleyan University Press, 1968), p. 104. Contrast the Japanese view of art versus technique: "The cardinal principle of Japanese dancing is natural movement with no straining of form. . . . To display your skill will deform your dance" (Scott, *Kabuki Theatre*, pp. 86-87).

9. For recitals and dates of first performance of the various dances see Appendix 3.

10. *New York Times*, 7 Dec. 1916, p. 11.

11. *New York Tribune*, 7 Dec. 1916, p. 3. Pavlova, famous for a dainty toe dance to this music, is reported to have expressed admiration for Ito's virile interpretation performed only with arms and upper body and is said to have called for it as an encore in a New York theater (Japanese Concert Program, April 1931).

12. Apparently all types of music interpretation come in for this kind of prejudice. Leonard Bernstein, in a recent television interview, said that he learned from Koussevitsky "the right of a conductor to his own personal connection with the composer."

13. Maisel, *Griffes*, p. 207; *New York Times*, 10 July 1917, p. 13; 5 Aug. Sec. VIII, p. 5; 21 Aug., p. 7; *New York Tribune*, 21 Aug. 1917, p. 9; 22 Aug., p. 9; 26 Aug., Sec. IV, p. 2; *Theatre Arts Magazine* (May 1917), p. 198.
Among the patronesses were Elsa Maxwell, Mrs. Harry Payne Whitney, Mrs. W. H. Vanderbilt, and Mrs. Percy Belmont. Settings and costumes were after designs by Willy Pogany, Livingston Platt, and John Wenger. There were special musical scores for Ito's dances by Charles T. Griffes, played by an orchestra under the direction of Marcel Ansotte.

14. *Kairn of Koridwen*; see Maisel, *Griffes*, pp. 183-189.

15. Ibid., pp. 202, 204; Marion Bauer, "Charles T. Griffes as I Remember Him," *Musical Quarterly* (1943), p. 369.

16. Maisel, *Griffes*, pp. 202, 254.

17. Ibid., pp. 202, 206, 210.

18. Griffes' words were: "Japanese music should not be too largely infused with Western ideas and procedures; yet Michio Ito himself, who understands the music of his native land *au fond*, believes that it will gain breadth of expression, that its beauties will be more widely understood if brought into modified contact with Western influences" (Frederick Martens, "Folk Music in the *Ballet Intime*," *New Music Review* [19 Oct. 1917], pp. 764-765); see also Maisel, *Griffes*, p. 206.

19. Maisel, *Griffes*, pp. 204-205; cf. Martens, "Folk Music," pp. 764-765.

20. Maisel, *Griffes*, pp. 159-160, 171-175, 187, 199, 201, 211, 232-233.

21. Ibid., p. 208; cf. pp. 211-215, 228-230, 234-235. See also Helen Ingersoll's comment (in *Theatre Arts Monthly* [Aug. 1928], p. 591) on the critics' revulsion to the Lewisohn "orchestral dramas" done to music by Bloch and Debussy: "It is however worth noting that these same musical values were more highly esteemed by the resisting critics when they were heard combined with the stage expression than they had been when heard alone."

22. Maisel, *Griffes*, pp. 209-210.

23. *New York Tribune*, 3 Feb. 1918, Sec. IV, p. 3; 17 Feb., Sec. IV, p. 2.

24. *Christian Science Monitor*, 2 March 1918, p. 22; Maisel, *Griffes*, pp. 229-230; Bauer, "Charles T. Griffes," pp. 355-409.

25. Maisel, *Griffes*, p. 234; cf. *New York Tribune*, 7 April 1918, Sec. IV, pp. 2, 6; 14 April, p. 2; *New York Times*, 14 April 1918, Sec. IV, p. 5.

26. See Maisel, *Griffes*, pp. 171, 231, 264.

27. Ibid., pp. 264-267; *New York Times*, 23 June 1919, p. 10.

28. *New York Tribune*, 7 April 1918, Sec. IV, pp. 2, 6. Four of these Yamada pieces were published the following year (1919) by Carl Fischer: "Crane and

168

ABOVE: Ito clowning during rehearsal on theater roof New York 1919.
*This type of movement was not used by Michio Ito
in any of his dances*

OPPOSITE PAGE: Ito in sheik's costume   *1928*

Tortoise," "Four Seasons in Kyoto," "Song of the Plovers," and "Kappore." A fifth, "The Blue Flame," was published in 1922 by Oliver Ditson. Two composers of lesser note—Leo Ornstein and Lassalle Spier—also accompanied the dancers on this program, playing their own compositions.

29. *New York Times*, 10 Feb. 1918, Sec. V, p. 8; *New York Tribune*, 3 March 1918, Sec. IV, p. 6; *Theatre Arts Monthly* (Feb. 1918), p. 111.

30. Staging and performance are more fully described in reviews of *Tamura's* revival in January 1921: see *Christian Science Monitor*, 1 Feb. 1921, p. 12; *New York Times*, 9 Jan. 1921, Sec. I, p. 2.

31. Maisel, *Griffes*, p. 231. It might be noted that Ito's friend and colleague Adolph Bolm used this technique in his production of *Coq d'Or* for the Metropolitan Opera; for description and opinions of the press, see *Current Opinion* (April 1918), p. 255; cf. Griffes' letter in Maisel, *Griffes*, p. 231.

32. *New York Times*, 7 July 1918, Sec. III, p. 3; *New York Tribune*, 11 July 1918, p. 11; Ito, "Memories." Dulac's costumes, masks, and cloth were on exhibit in a New York art gallery (William Butler Yeats, *Letters*, ed. Allan Wade [London: R. Hart-Davis, 1954], 22 March 1920, to Edmund Dulac; Wade's note is apparently not completely accurate). Ito was not satisfied with Dulac's music (see his "Memories").

33. For details see excerpts from Griffes' letters in Maisel, *Griffes*, pp. 243-244; *New York Times*, 7 July 1918, Sec. III, p. 3.

34. *New York Tribune*, 19 Aug. 1917, Sec. IV, p. 2.

35. Ezra Pound and Ernest Fenollosa, *The Classic Noh Theatre of Japan* (New York: New Directions Paperback, 1959), p. 69; cf. Arthur Waley, *The Nō Plays of Japan with Letters by Oswald Sickert* (New York: Grove Press, 1957), pp. 53, 309 (Sickert letter).

36. Elizabeth Selden, *The Dancer's Quest* (Berkeley: University of California Press, 1935), p. 84.

37. Most of the information on dances performed in New York (1916-1929) is derived from newspaper and periodical accounts, which are seldom complete.

38. A revue in two acts and twelve scenes by Philip Bartholomeu and John Murray Anderson; music by A. Baldwin Sloane; at the Greenwich Village Theater, July 15, 1919. See *New York Times*, 16 July 1919, p. 14, and Heywood Broun's review in *New York Tribune*, 16 July, p. 9.

39. Hugh Abercrombie Anderson, *Out without My Rubbers: The Memoirs of John Murray Anderson* (New York: Library Publishers, 1954), letter to Anderson from Otto Kahn, pp. 65-66.

40. Musical comedy in two parts; book and lyrics by John Murray Anderson, Anna Wynne O'Ryan, and Jack Yellen; music by Milton Ager; at Maxine Elliott's Theater, 19 March 1920.

41. *Christian Science Monitor*, 24 March 1920, p. 17; cf. reviews by Heywood Broun, *New York Tribune*, 20 March 1920, p. 11; 28 March, Sec. III, p. 1.

42. A revue first presented by Richard G. Herndon, 15 June 1922, at the Earl Carroll Theater with Raymond Hitchcock and Frank Fay also in the cast. Reviewers remarked the incongruity of joining Ito's "art" with Hitchcock and Fay's crude "Broadway humor." The revue soon closed but reopened at the Little Theater, 31 July, without Hitchcock and Fay and with "superb" effect, as can be seen from the

criticism quoted herewith. Cf. Percy Hammond, *New York Tribune*, 16 June 1922, p. 10.

43. *New York Tribune*, 1 Aug. 1922, p. 6.

44. *New York Times*, 1 Aug. 1922, p. 14.

45. *New York Tribune*, 6 Aug. 1922, Sec. V, p. 1.

46. *New York Times*, 16 June 1922, p. 20.

47. *Christian Science Monitor*, 8 Aug. 1922, p. 6.

48. A drama in three acts by John Masefield, produced by the Theatre Guild; directed by Augustin Duncan; at the Garrick Theater, 13 Oct. 1919; settings by Lee Simonson; technical advice by Michio Ito. See *New York Tribune*, 26 Oct. 1919, Sec. IV, p. 6; 5 Oct., Sec. IV, p. 6; *New York Times*, 14 Oct. 1919, p. 14.

49. Heywood Broun in *New York Tribune*, 14 Oct. 1919, p. 11; cf. ibid., 19 Oct. 1919, Sec. IV, p. 5; *Review* (New York), 1 Nov. 1919, p. 545; *New Republic*, 12 Nov. 1919, pp. 326-327.

50. A musical play by Cloyd Head and Eunice Tietjens; music by Ruth White Warfield; staged by Norman Bel Geddes; dance direction by Michio Ito; produced by Richard G. Herndon at the National Theater, 20 Oct. 1925. See *New York Times*, 21 Oct. 1925, p. 20.

51. *Theatre Arts Monthly* (Jan. 1926), pp. 33-34; cf. *Theatre* (Dec. 1925), p. 44.

52. Stark Young in *New Republic*, 11 Nov. 1925, pp. 305-306. This review strongly disapproves of the play, the principal actors, and the direction of the drama proper.

53. *Sister Beatrice (Soeur Béatrice)* by Maurice Maeterlinck. I was unable to find the date and place of performance.

54. Marie Eisenbrant, "A Study in Stage Sets from Belasco to Bakst," *Dance Magazine* (Aug. 1927), pp. 10, 11, 53.

55. A play in five acts by Franz Werfel; trans. Ruth Langner; directed by Jacob Ben-Ami; settings and costumes by Lee Simonson; dance direction by Michio Ito; produced by the Theatre Guild at the Guild Theater, 25 Jan. 1926.

56. *New York Times*, 7 Feb. 1926, Sec. VII, p. 1. Compare this description with that of Ito's "Demon" performed at his March 1917 dance concert as "a harpy of shadows snatched upward by a whirlwind before the eyes of astonished beholders" (*New York Times*, 8 March 1917, p. 9). See also review of *Goat Song* headline, "Color, acting and fine direction leave spectators spellbound" (*New York Tribune*, 26 Jan. 1926, p. 19).

57. *Turandot*, a play by Carl Gozzi, in a Yiddish version; staged by Boris Glagolin; dances by Michio Ito; presented by the Habima Players at the Manhattan Opera Playhouse, 11 Jan. 1929.

58. *New York Times*, 12 Jan. 1929, p. 14.

59. Musical play in three acts adapted from *The Willow Tree* by J. Harry Benrimo and Harrison Rhodes; book and lyrics by Harry B. Smith; score by Sigmund Romberg; dances by Michio Ito; presented by Messrs. Shubert at the Forty-fourth Street Theater, 28 March 1927.

60. *Dance Magazine* (May 1927), p. 59.

61. *New York Times,* 29 March 1927, p. 22.

62. *The Mikado,* an opera in two acts; words by W. S. Gilbert and music by Arthur Sullivan; staged by Winthrop Ames; settings and costumes by Raymond Sovey; dances by Michio Ito; presented by Winthrop Ames' Gilbert and Sullivan Opera Company at the Royale Theater, 17 Sept. 1927.

63. J. Brooks Atkinson in *New York Times,* 19 Sept. 1927, p. 30.

64. George Goldsmith in *New York Herald-Tribune,* 19 Sept. 1927, p. 12. He also recounts that he saw across the aisle Mr. Gabriel of the *Sun,* Atkinson of the *Times,* Anderson of the *Post,* and Allen of *Women's Wear,* all enjoying themselves and muttering encomiums.

65. John Mason Brown, "The Dull Devil of Melodrama—Broadway in Review," *Theatre Arts Monthly* (Nov. 1927), pp. 825-826.

66. Puccini's *Madame Butterfly,* presented in English by the American Opera Company; musical direction by Vladmir Rosing; dramatic direction by Michio Ito; settings by Norman Edwards; costumes designed and executed by Yuji Ito. The opera opened in Washington, D.C., on 13 Dec. 1927 and in New York at the Gallo Theater on 11 Jan. 1928.
   Yuji Ito (1897-1963), brother of Michio, came to New York as a singer in 1917, had a role in Michio's *Pinwheel Revel,* and later became a designer of costumes and masks for stage and films. See *New York Times,* 4 Nov. 1963, p. 35; *Japan Times,* 26 Nov. 1939, p. 6; 3 Dec. p. 8; 4 Dec. p. 4.

67. *New York Herald-Tribune,* 12 Jan. 1928, p. 24.

68. *New York Times,* 8 Jan. 1928, Sec. VIII, p. 10.

69. *The Story of the Soldier (L'Histoire du Soldat),* a narrative in five scenes to be read, played, and danced; music by Igor Stravinsky; dialogue and narrative by C. F. Ramuz; orchestra conducted by Pierre Monteux; drama and pantomime directed by Michio Ito; scenery and costumes designed by Donald Oenslager; presented by the League of Composers at the Jolson (now Century) Theater, 25 March 1928.

70. Irving Weil, "'Soldier' Given with Pantomimic Rite," *Musical America* (31 March 1928), pp. 1, 7.

71. *Thirty-three Years of American Dance, 1927-1959, and the American Ballet* (Pittsfield, Mass.: privately printed, 1959), p. 13. For a list of dances see Appendix 3.

72. *The Fox's Grave (Kitsune Zuka).* For complete English text see *Outlook,* 133 (14 Feb. 1923), 306-308. P. 306 has illustration showing Ito as the servant Tarokaja. The English text of *She Who Was Fished (Tsuri Onna),* another kyōgen translated by Ito and Ledoux, appears in *Outlook,* 133 (31 Jan. 1923), 218-219. A third one, *Somebody Nothing (Busu),* appears in *Asia,* 21 (Dec. 1921), 1011-1012.

73. E.g., with Benjamin Zemach, 25 Sept. 1928; in Irene Lewisohn's production of "orchestral dramas," 4 May 1928.

74. John Martin, "Project of Michio Ito for Theatre Building is Taking Shape," *New York Times,* 10 June 1928, Sec. VIII, p. 7; Michio Ito letter to editor, *New York Herald-Tribune,* 18 March 1928, Sec. VII, p. 10. See also *Herald-Tribune,* 25 March 1928, Sec. VII, p. 10; Nickolas Muray, "Plans for a Theatre of the Dance," *Dance Magazine* (Nov. 1928), pp. 39, 58; *Los Angeles Times,* 28 April 1929, "Music," p. 12; *Los Angeles Times,* 2 June 1929, p. 13.

75. *Dance Magazine* (Feb. 1929), p. 63; cf. *New York Herald-Tribune*, 6 Feb. 1928, p. 11; 19 March, p. 13; *New York Times*, 1 April 1928, Sec. IX, p. 5.

76. For Lester Horton see Jacques Baril, *Dictionnaire de Danse* (Paris: Edition du Seuil, 1964), s.v. "Horton, Lester"; or Anatol Chujoy and P. W. Manchester, *Dance Encyclopedia* (New York: Simon and Schuster, 1967), s.v. "Horton, Lester"; for Nimura see *New York Times*, 5 Feb. 1928, p. 5; for Angna Enters, ibid; also see Ruth Pickering, "Michio Ito," *Nation*, 16 Jan. 1929, pp. 88, 90; for Pauline Koner, see Chujoy and Manchester, *Dance Encyclopedia*, s.v. "Koner, Pauline."

77. *Theatre Magazine* (April 1929), p. 41; cf. *New York Times*, 16 Sept. 1928, Sec. IX, p. 7.

IV. *California and the Symphonies*

1. The dancers, besides Ito, were Dorothy Wagner, who also assisted him in his teaching, Estelle Reed, and Georgia Graham. For the effect of the program on others see Isabel Morse Jones, "Ito's Art Entrances," *Los Angeles Times*, 29 April 1929, Sec. II, p. 7.

2. Edith Jane School of Dancing on Highland Avenue.

3. Laurence Binyon, *Painting in the Far East*, 3d ed. (New York: Dover, 1959), p. 272.

4. Cf. Isabel Morse Jones in *Los Angeles Times*, 2 June 1929, p. 13.

5. See M. W.'s complaint that "this unique and brilliant artist" does not himself do his new numbers but leaves the task to his assisting artists (*New York Herald-Tribune*, 19 March 1928, p. 13).

6. *Somebody Nothing*. Players: Ralph Matson, Lester Horton, and Thomas de Graffenreid. For text of translation see *Asia* (Dec. 1921), pp. 1011-1012. *The Fox's Grave* with the same cast; text of translation in *Outlook*, 14 Feb. 1923, pp. 306-308.

7. Lewis Barrington, on leave from his position as art curator at the Smithsonian Institute, had come to California to assist Ito, with whom he had previously worked in New York.

8. Ito, the harpist, and the chorus of three women (under Ito's direction) made their own costumes out of a heavy, black sateen: a simple shirt with kimono sleeves, a skirt made of some six yards of material, tight in back and folded into many pleats in front with the excess width tucked in at the waist. The headdress, of the same material, was not much more complicated. The "cloth" that the chorus unfolded and folded was a long piece of the same sateen, two yards wide. The old man's costume was multicolored; it had been dyed by Lester Horton. He cut it into ribbons on the actor. I remember his asking, "Have I got enough shredded wheat?"

9. Details of the production are to be found in the *Pasadena Star News*, 3 Sept. 1929, Sec. II, p. 15; 5 Sept., p. 9; 7 Sept., p. 2; 10 Sept., p. 2; 12 Sept., p. 3; 13 Sept., p. 11; 14 Sept., p. 15; 16 Sept., p. 9; 18 Sept., Sec. II, p. 13; 20 Sept., p. 1; 21 Sept., Sec. II, p. 13.

10. For a good discussion of the "orchestral dramas" and what the form accomplishes, see *Theatre Arts Monthly* (June 1928), pp. 381-382; (Aug. 1928), pp. 591-594, and the various newspaper criticisms of the performance.

11. Dalcroze's idea is perhaps best expressed by his friend and collaborator Adolphe Appia, who is quoted and explained by Walter R. Volbach (in *Adolphe*

Appia, a Prophet of the Modern Theatre: A Profile [Middletown, Conn.: Wesleyan University Press, 1968], p. 169): "'In space, units of time are expressed by a succession of forms, hence by movement. In time, space is expressed by a succession of words and sounds, that is to say by varying time-durations prescribing the extent of movement.' Appia insists on movement as the unifier of dramatic art which thus creates the ideal form. In relating music, the element of time, to space, movement functions as the main catalyst of the whole."

12. Dalcroze's realization of the idea was far from perfect. For example, in the Hellerau *Orpheus*, conception and execution, for which Dalcroze was responsible, were somewhat less applauded than the staging, which was by Appia and Salzmann (see Volbach, *Adolphe Appia*, pp. 89-92). Both Dalcroze and the Lewisohns introduced realistic drama into their productions, and both were criticized for ruining the music by so doing. Ito, on the contrary, did realize the idea that music is the direct expression of emotion and that bodily movement, through *symbolic* gesture, is the indirect expression.

13. *Pasadena Star News*, 20 Sept. 1929, p. 1.

14. Tournament of Roses Association in *Pasadena Star News*, 5 Sept. 1929, p. 9.

15. Ibid., 21 Sept. 1929, Sec. II, p. 13.

16. Kisaku Ito (1899-1967), stage designer, president of Haiyūza Theater, author of *Study of Stage Setting* and other books, known in the United States for settings of films such as *Gate of Hell*, and for sets of the Azuma Kabuki company.

17. As noted earlier, Ito always worked out a dance in complete detail before either performing or teaching it. For his symphony interpretations he prepared large charts (14″ × 20″) on which he entered, beneath the musical notation, notation and sketches for particular gestures and notation for group movement. That is, the whole choreography had been conceived and worked out in detail before he began to teach it to the dancers. Molinari was fascinated by these charts.

18. Patterson Greene in *Los Angeles Examiner*, 16 Aug. 1930, p. 8.

19. Richard Drake Saunders in *Hollywood News*, 16 Aug. 1930.

20. Charles Daggett in *Los Angeles Record*, 16 Aug. 1930. This review seems to imply that Ito was one of the dancers. He was not.

21. Presented by the Redlands Community Music Association (as the 489th concert in its thirteenth season) in cooperation with the Federal Music Project; symphony orchestra and chorus conducted by Vernon Robinson; principal singers, Clemence Gifford (Orpheus), Ruth La Gourgue (Eurydice), and Genevieve Young (Amor).

Contemporary notices and reviews referred to the dancing as "pantomime," but there was no attempt at pantomime. Dalcroze, for his *Orpheus*, had taught dancing to the singers for six months prior to the performance—without much success, according to the reviews—and even his regular, trained dancers were overly realistic and not always in accord with the music's "idea." Michio Ito, on the other hand, placed all the music—orchestra, chorus, and principal singers—out of sight; the dancers alone interpreted the music visually with formal gesture.

22. *Japan Biographical Encyclopedia and Who's Who*, 3d ed., 1964-1965 (Tokyo: Rengo Press), s.v. "Konoye, Hidemaro." Also shortly before rehearsals started and after much consultation with Ito, Leopold Stokowski recorded the Konoye *Etenraku* with his Philadelphia Orchestra for the Victor Company.

23. On 24 Sept. 1937, with Adolf Tandler conducting.

24. *Musical Courier*, 3 Nov. 1927, p. 40.

25. *Japan Times* (Tokyo), 17 April 1931, pp. 1, 8.

26. Ibid.

27. Ibid.

28. For a partial list of concerts in California see Appendix 3.

29. *Mary Magdalene*, with chorus and orchestra conducted by the composer; costumes and setting designed and executed by Kisaku Ito; first presented on 19 Jan. 1931 in the Pasadena Playhouse.

30. *No, No, Nanette*, First National Studio, 26 Feb. 1930; musical in color adapted from the musical comedy by Frank Mandel, Otto Harbach, Vincent Youmans et al; director Clarence Badger. Michio Ito choreographed and directed a dance sequence based on the Japanese myth of the goddess Amaterasu. This film is not to be confused with a later (1940) version of *No, No, Nanette* made by RKO Pictures.
Madame Butterfly, Paramount Productions, 5 Jan. 1933; based on a story by John Luther Long and on the play by David Belasco; director Marion Gering; starring Sylvia Sidney, Cary Grant, Charles Ruggles, Irving Pichel, and Helen Jerome Eddy. Ito was responsible for technical direction of costumes, manners, movement, etc., and as usual the visual quality found favor: "In costuming, makeup and settings the film is quaintly satisfying and the photography has charm" (*New York Times*, 26 Dec. 1932, p. 26).
Booloo, Paramount Pictures, 22 July 1938; direction and story, Clyde E. Elliott; starring Colin Tapley, Jayne Regan, Michio Ito, and Herbert de Souza. Ito also acted in a technical capacity. This film also received favorable reviews (e.g., *New York Times*, 30 July 1938, p. 10).

31. *La Traviata* by Verdi, performed at Los Angeles Philharmonic Auditorium, Oct. 25 and 27, 1936; producer, Max Rabinoff; conductor, Albert Conti; chorus master, Aldo Franchetti; ballet director, Michio Ito.

32. Tokujiro Tsutsui and his Company of Players in *Samurai and Geisha* with classical Japanese dramas adapted and directed by Michio Ito; opened in Los Angeles at the Figueroa Playhouse, 10 Feb. 1930; in New York at the Booth Theater, 4 March 1930, under the auspices of the Theatre Guild. For description of performances see *Los Angeles Times*, 9 Feb. 1930, Sec. III, p. 14 (review by Edwin Schallert), 12 Feb., Sec. II, p. 11; *New York Times* (review by J. Brooks Atkinson), 5 March 1930, p. 26.
The Japanese Children's Theatre in Kabuki Plays and Dances, Wilshire Ebell Theater, Los Angeles, 15 Jan. 1932.

33. At Koyasan Betsuin Hall, Los Angeles. Michio Ito had previously created dances for Teiko, for their 1939-40 visit to Japan, when she performed in dance concerts with him and in his Japanese translation of *At the Hawk's Well* (see chap. ii, n. 79, above). During that visit Ito also directed *Daibutsu Kaigan* ("The Opening of Buddha's Eyes"), a historical play by Hideo Nagata, presented at Tsukiji Playhouse, Tokyo. The décor was by Michio's brother Kisaku Ito, the costumes by their brother Yuji; a third brother, the actor Koreya Senda, was a member of the production's distinguished cast, and Teiko performed a dance, composed by Michio Ito, on a huge Buddha's hand.

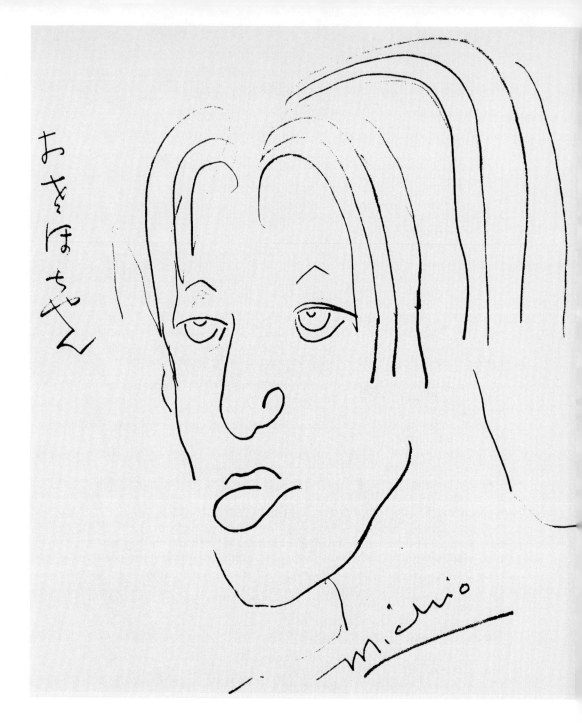

おきほちゃん

ABOVE:
Michio Ito, self-caricature   1937
Inscribed to "Saoko" (Cecilia Nakamura)

OPPOSITE: Costume sketch for Passepied by Michio Ito

Index

Boldface type indicates pages on which illustrations appear.

E-flat and in C-sharp minor (dances), 86, 110, 122

Clark, Allan, **51**

Claudel, Paul, 158 n. 8

Coliseum theater (London), 37, 42, 158 n. 3

Comedy, 7, 26

Community dance, 79, 85

Cornell, Katharine, 55

Costume, 7, 11, 12, 24, 34, 86, 91, 95-96, 98, 163 n. 47, 173 n. 8

Craig, (Edward) Gordon, 44-45, 49, 56

Crane and Tortoise (Tsuru Kame), 17, 20

Cunard, Lady Emerald, 40, 49, 161 n. 17

Daibutsu Kaigan (The Opening of Buddha's Eyes), 175 n. 33

Dalcroze, Émile Jaques-, 4, 38-39, 40, 41, 55-56, 86, 157 n. 47, 158 n. 8, 173-174 nn. 11-12, 174 n. 21

Dance: definition of, 3, 4-5, 27-28 (*see also* Ito, Michio, dance composition); Japanese and occidental, 37, 98, 105

Dance poems, 3, 4-5, 69, 77, 105, 155 n. 1; *Arabesque II*, 24, **25,** 26, 28; *Ball*, 3-4, 27, 57, 61, 155 n. 2; *Caresse*, 8-9, **10;** *Caucasian Dance*, 12; *Chopin Étude*, 22, **23;** *Dō-Jō-Jī*, 65; *Ecclesiastique I*, 4, 79; *II*, 116; *IV*, **100,** 116; *Faun*, 7, 12; *Fox*, 42, **43,** 65, 69; *Gnossienne I and II*, 20; *Golliwogg's Cakewalk*, 24; *Greek Warrior*, 20; *Habanera*, 11, 12, 13; *Hawk* (Guardian of the well), 45, **46, 47,** 48, 53, 54, 165 n. 79; *Impression of a Chinese Actor*, 13, **19;** *Japanese Spring Dance*, 13; *Javanese*, 12, 34; *Joy*; 22; *Ladybug*, 22; *Little Shepherdess*, 24, **97;** *Lotus Land*, 21; *Maid with the Flaxen Hair*, 24, 25; *Minuet*, 11, 34; *Pair of Fans*, 13, 17, **18;** *Passepied*, 11, **177;** *Pavane*, 11-12; *Pizzicati*, 57, **58, 59, 60,** 79, 88, 91; *Prelude V*, 7-8, 28; *VI*, 8; *VIII*, 8; *IX*, 8, 28; *X*, 8; *Sakura-Sakura*, 64; *Shō-Jō (The Spirit of Wine)*, 61, 65, 69; *Single Fan*, 13, 17; *Spanish Fan*, 12; *Spring Rain*, 13, 17, **18,** 118; *Tango*, 12, **14-16,** 34; *Tone Poem I*, 5, 7, 26, 27; *II*, 5, **6,** 7, 20, 26, 27; *III* (*see Faun*); *Tragedy*, 20-21, 26, **84;** *White Peacock*, 21-22, 27, 29. For additional dances see Appendixes 1 and 3.

180   Dancers' Guild, 77

Debussy, Claude, 24-26, 38, 41, 86, 161 n. 19

Dō-Jō-Jī, 65

Donkey, The, 126, 131

Dulac, Edmond. *See* Dulac, Edmund

Dulac, Edmund, **46, 47,** 48, 49, 53, 65, 86, 163 n. 47, 170 n. 32

Duncan, Elizabeth, 38

Duncan, Isadora, 38

Dvorak, Anton, 86, **87,** 122

Ecclesiastique I, 4, 79; *II*, 116; *III*, 123; *IV*, **100,** 116

Egyptian influence, 38, 45, **46,** 48

Eliot, T(homas) S(tearns), 50, 157 n. 34

Ellington, Duke (Edward Kennedy Ellington), 35

Enters, Angna, 77, 78

Epstein, Jacob, 39

Etenraku, 96, 98, **100, 101,** 174 n. 22

Eurythmics. *See* Dalcroze, Émile Jaques-

Evil, 3, 4, 5, 8

Fable. *See* Idea and fable

Faithful, The (Masefield,) 70, **73**

Fan. *See* Symbols, fan

Faun, 7, 12

Fenollosa, Ernest, 42, 44, 45, 69, 161 n. 26, 162 n. 28

Form, 7, 8-9, 10-11, 12, 42; and line, 34; and restraint, 166 n. 8; and stylization, 28, 48, 174 n. 21; suggestion of space, 4, 34. *See also* Idea and fable

Foujita, Tsuguharu, 39, 161 n. 11

Foundation of theatric arts, 77

Fox (dance), 42, **43,** 65, 69

Fox's Grave, The (Kitsune Zuka), 77

Fujita. *See* Foujita

Gardner, Helen, 26

Genée, Adeline, 37

Genroku period, 13

Gesture, 5, 28-29, 34, 48; final, 5, 7, 29; initial, 29; Ten Gestures, 29, **30-31, 32, 33,** Appendix 4. *See also* Form

Gilbert and Sullivan (*The Mikado*), 75-76

Gilman, Laurence, 56

Gluck, Christoph Willibald: *Orpheus*, 96, 174 n. 21

Gnossiennes I and II, 20

Goat Song, 75

183

184